Bigfoot

FACT OR FICTION?

CREATURE SCENE INVESTIGATION

Bigfoot

FACT OR FICTION?

Rick Emmer

CHELSEA HOUSE
PUBLISHERS
An imprint of Infobase Publishing

BIGFOOT: FACT OR FICTION?

Copyright © 2010 by Infobase Publishing

Chelsea House
An imprint of Infobase Publishing
132 West 31st Street
New York NY 10001

Library of Congress Cataloging-in-Publication Data

Emmer, Rick.
  Bigfoot: fact or fiction? / Rick Emmer.
      p. cm. — (Creature scene investigation)
  Includes bibliographical references and index.
  ISBN 978-0-7910-9778-6 (hardcover)
  1. Sasquatch—Juvenile literature. I. Title. II. Series.
  QL89.2.S2E46 2010
  001.944—dc22   2009011468

Chelsea House books are available at special discounts when purchased in bulk
quantities for businesses, associations, institutions, or sales promotions. Please call our
Special Sales Department in New York at (212) 967-8800 or (800) 322-8755.

You can find Chelsea House on the World Wide Web at
http://www.chelseahouse.com

Text design by James Scotto-Lavino, Erik Lindstrom
Cover design by Takeshi Takahashi
Composition by Facts on File
Cover printed by Bang Printing, Brainerd, Minn.
Book printed and bound by Bang Printing, Brainerd, Minn.
Date printed: January, 2010
Printed in the United States of America

10 9 8 7 6 5 4 3 2 1

This book is printed on acid-free paper.

All links and Web addresses were checked and verified to be correct at the time of publication. Because of the dynamic nature of the Web, some addresses and links may have
changed since publication and may no longer be valid.

CONTENTS

PREFACE

Welcome to Creature Scene Investigation: The Science of Cryptozoology, the series devoted to the science of **cryptozoology**. Bernard Heuvelmans, a French scientist, invented that word 50 years ago. It is a combination of the words *kryptos* (Greek for "hidden") and *zoology*, the scientific study of animals. So, cryptozoology is the study of "hidden" animals, or **cryptids**, which are animals that some people believe may exist, even though it is not yet proven.

Just how does a person prove that a particular cryptid exists? Dedicated cryptozoologists (the scientists who study cryptozoology) follow a long, two-step process as they search for cryptids. First, they gather as much information about their animal as they can. The most important sources of information are people who live near where the cryptid supposedly lives. These people are most familiar with the animal and the stories about it. So, for example, if cryptozoologists want to find out about the Loch Ness Monster, they must ask the people who live around Loch Ness, a lake in Scotland where the monster was sighted. If they want to learn about Bigfoot, they should talk to people who found its footprints or took its photo.

A cryptozoologist carefully examines all of this information. This is important because it helps the scientist identify and rule out some stories that might be mistakes or lies. The remaining information can then be used to produce a clear scientific description of the cryptid in question. It might even lead to solid proof that the cryptid exists.

Second, a cryptozoologist takes the results of his or her research and goes into the field to look for solid evidence that the cryptid really exists. The best possible evidence would be an actual **specimen**—maybe even a live one. Short of that, a combination of good videos, photographs, footprints, body parts (bones and teeth, for example), and other clues can make a strong case for a cryptid's existence.

In this way, the science of cryptozoology is a lot like **forensics**, the science made famous by all of those crime investigation shows on TV. The goal of forensics detectives is to use the evidence they find to catch a criminal. The goal of cryptozoologists is to catch a cryptid—or at least to find solid evidence that it really exists.

Some cryptids have become world-famous. The most famous ones of all are probably the legendary Loch Ness Monster of Scotland and the apelike Bigfoot of the United States. There are many other cryptids out there, too. At least, some people think so.

This series explores the legends and lore—the facts and the fiction—behind the most popular of all of the cryptids: the gigantic shark known as Megalodon, Kraken the monster squid, an African dinosaur called Mokele-mbembe, the Loch Ness Monster, and Bigfoot. This series also takes a look at some lesser-known but equally fascinating cryptids from around the world:

- the mysterious, blood-sucking Chupacabras, or "goat sucker," from the Caribbean, Mexico, and South America
- the Sucuriju, a giant anaconda snake from South America
- Megalania, the gigantic monitor lizard from Australia
- the Ropen and Kongamato, prehistoric flying reptiles from Africa and the island of New Guinea
- the thylacine, or Tasmanian wolf, from the island of Tasmania

- the Ri, a mermaidlike creature from the waters of New Guinea
- the thunderbird, a giant vulture from western North America

Some cryptids, such as dinosaurs like Mokele-mbembe, are animals already known to science. These animals are thought to have become extinct. Some people, however, believe that these animals are still alive in lands that are difficult for most humans to reach. Other cryptids, such as the giant anaconda snake, are simply unusually large (or, in some cases, unusually small) versions of modern animals. And yet other cryptids, such as the Chupacabras, appear to be animals right out of a science fiction movie, totally unlike anything known to modern science.

As cryptozoologists search for these unusual animals, they keep in mind a couple of slogans. The first is, "If it sounds too good to be true, it probably isn't true." The second is, "Absence of proof is not proof of absence." The meaning of these slogans will become clear as you observe how cryptozoologists analyze and interpret the evidence they gather in their search for these awesome animals.

MEET BIGFOOT

Accounts of Bigfoot in America go back as far as
this land is mentioned in history, and in legends
and folklore long before that.... The truth is that
at least one unknown species of primate exists in
America. It's a big story and it's not getting the
attention it deserves.

—Loren Coleman,
Bigfoot: The True Story of Apes in America

The five gold miners huddled in their tiny cabin. They
were trapped. It was the middle of the night, and
monstrous creatures outside were trying to break in. The
beasts were big and powerful. They heaved heavy rocks and
boulders against the sides of the cabin and onto the roof.
They pounded on the walls as they tried to get to the men
inside.

The miners fought back, shooting their guns through the walls and roof, hoping to scare off the attackers. At one point, a huge, hairy arm punched through a gap between two logs in one of the walls. Its hand grabbed an ax handle. As it tried to take the ax, one quick-thinking miner twisted the ax so it jammed against the wall. Then he fired his gun through the gap. The creature let go of the ax, but the attack continued. For five hours, the creatures bombarded the cabin. Then, as sunrise approached, the attack stopped and the creatures slipped away.

The year was 1924. The miners had been working in a gold mine on the eastern slope of Mount St. Helens in Washington State. The afternoon before the attack, two of the miners were collecting water from a nearby creek. One of them saw a huge, hairy, apelike creature watching them from a nearby hilltop. He shot at the beast five times but it ran away. This puzzled the miners, because the shooter was sure that all five shots had hit the creature—two in the back and three in the head.

The day after the nightmarish midnight attack, one of the miners saw another of the creatures jump out from behind a clump of bushes and start to run away. He shot the beast in the back as it reached the edge of a cliff overhanging a deep river gorge. It toppled over the cliff and disappeared in the swiftly moving water below.

After these incidents, the gorge was dubbed Ape Canyon. The miners' wild adventure has been retold as the legend of Ape Canyon, one of the most famous of all stories about the mysterious beast we call Bigfoot. This tale fires the imagination of every hiker, hunter, and lumberjack who enters the territory of the apelike beast of the Pacific Northwest region.

INTRODUCING BIGFOOT

The list of names goes on and on: Bigfoot, Sasquatch, Wild Man, Skunk Ape, Yeti, Yowie. . . . Probably no other ani-

This large footprint measuring almost 18 inches (46 cm) long was discovered in 1980 near Johnstown, Pennsylvania. Local residents reported strange noises and an unusual odor near where the print was found. The animal that left the print was never identified.

mal—real or imagined—is known by as many names as this mysterious, hairy beast with oversized feet.

Some cryptids have only been sighted a few times. Bigfoot and its footprints, on the other hand, have been reported many times by many people in many places. It would be difficult, if not impossible, to tally all the sightings. The number would surely run into the thousands.

Many of these reports are untrue. They might be hoaxes (jokes) or cases in which people honestly think they are seeing Bigfoot, but really are not. But even so, it is still interesting and informative to take a look at what people are saying about this mysterious creature. After all, reports of encounters of the hairy kind do not all come from jokers or overly excited hikers. Some perfectly cool, calm, and collected observers report sightings, too. These observers include scientists, foresters, and experienced outdoors people who are not likely to be fooled by a practical joke or to play a prank themselves. So, using a critical eye and a bit of common sense, let's take a look at what the eyewitnesses have reported.

Will the Real Bigfoot Please Stand Up?

Since Bigfoot owes its name to the big footprints it leaves behind, let's start by taking a look at the variety of prints described by eyewitnesses.

Bigfoot prints come in many sizes. This is not surprising, since there have been thousands and thousands of footprints reported all over the United States and half of Canada. If Bigfoot exists, there is no way a single creature could stomp around and make all of those prints, even if it worked nonstop, every single second of the year. If Bigfoot is a real creature, there can't be just one. There must be one or more groups of Bigfoot; in other words, populations made up of smaller youngsters and bigger adults, just like populations of humans. That means smaller footprints as well as bigger footprints.

Bigfoot prints found in snow, dirt, and mud range from 11 to 24 inches long (28 to 61 centimeters) and 4 to 12 inches wide (10 to 30 cm). Those are all pretty big footprints, and the wide range in size is exactly what would be expected if there were a whole population of Bigfoot out there. (This book follows the common practice of using the term *Bigfoot* for the plural form as well as the singular form.)

It is more than the sizes of the footprints that make them stand out. They are also remarkable because they look like huge, fat, flat-footed human footprints. Most Bigfoot prints are extremely flat-footed, meaning that they do not have an empty space in the print where the foot's arch would be. Many prints also have five humanlike toes. Some have an extra-large big toe that points inward, making it look like a gorilla's footprint.

These footprint casts were part of a Bigfoot exhibit at the Idaho Museum of Natural History. In addition to being unusually large, these footprints were made by feet that had little or no arch.

Other prints have only four toes, but that may be because the pinkie toe didn't press hard enough on the ground to leave an impression. That appears in human prints, too. Then there are the three-toed, dinosaurlike prints found in Southern California as well as in the small town of Fouke, Arkansas. (These prints were the inspiration for the "Fouke Monster" in the 1973 film *The Legend of Boggy Creek*.) Many of these three-toed prints also have a V-shaped bottom, like the keel running along the bottom of a boat. This would be very unstable to walk on, so it's highly unlikely that a creature with such a foot exists.

A Portrait of the Beast

Journalist John Green has put together hundreds of eyewitness reports from all over the United States and western Canada for his book *Sasquatch: The Apes Among Us*. In

A gorilla foot is much flatter and has toes that are noticeably different from a human foot.

general, these reports describe a huge, hairy, apelike beast 8
or 9 feet tall (roughly 3 meters) with a gorillalike face, including a big, flat nose and a head shaped like a cone or dome.

Weight estimates range from a few hundred pounds
to more than 1,000 pounds (455 kilograms). The animal is
almost always observed standing or walking upright on two
legs like a human. That means it is **bipedal**, as opposed to
quadrupedal (or four-legged) like a dog. Sometimes, however,
it is seen scooting around on all fours. Most reports describe

LET'S GET TECHNICAL: THE SAGITTAL CREST

People who claim to have seen Bigfoot often describe an animal with a big head shaped like a cone or dome. Some Bigfoot fans like to think this means the creature has a super-sized brain with special psychic powers. The shape of Bigfoot's head, however, can be explained in a better way: Just look at the head of the largest known **primate**, the adult male gorilla.

The sagittal crest is visible on the skull of this adult male gorilla.

The skull of a mature male gorilla has a vertical ridge of bone that is 1 to 2 inches high (2.5 to 5 cm) and runs along the middle of the top of the skull. This is called the **sagittal crest**, and it makes the gorilla's head look dome-shaped. The sides of the crest give extra surface area where the gorilla's huge chewing muscles attach to the skull. The lower end of each chewing muscle attaches to the lower jawbone. These massive muscles work together with other jaw muscles to provide tremendous chewing power, allowing the big ape to smash and grind the huge amounts of tough leaves and other plant materials that it eats every day. If these features are what people see on Bigfoot, it means this cryptid must be one big eater.

very brief encounters, because the animal, despite its scary appearance, seems to be afraid of people and ordinarily disappears into the woods as soon as it is spotted.

Many of Green's stories are a bit out of the ordinary—in fact, some are downright extraordinary. The animals described in some of these accounts are so hard to believe in that it is easy to see why many people don't take Bigfoot seriously. See for yourself:

- Bigfoot is always described as hairy, but the hair color ranges from white to reddish brown to medium brown to black. The only places where naked skin has been seen are on its face, palms, and the bottoms of its feet. Even the breasts of females are described as furry, a condition not seen among any known apes (gorillas, chimpanzees, orangutans, and gibbons).

- Descriptions of Bigfoot eyes vary in interesting ways. Daytime observers often describe Bigfoot's eyes as dark and beady. Many eyewitnesses who encounter Bigfoot at night claim that its eyes glow in the dark and appear red, pink, green, or white. The glow may be explained by a car's headlights reflecting off the backs of the creature's eyeballs. (A reflective surface called the *tapetum lucidum* lines the backs of the eyeballs in many **nocturnal** animals.) But often, the eyes are reported to glow on their own in total darkness, much like lightbulbs. This claim is not as far-fetched as it might seem. Although no known ape possesses **bioluminescent** ("glow-in-the-dark") eyes, such eyes do exist. For example, many fish that live in deep, dark ocean waters possess structures called **photophores**, located just beneath the eyeballs. Photophores produce light by means of a chemical reaction.

- Bigfoot stinks. Some observers of the beast claim that it smells really bad, like rotten eggs or cucumbers, or even like a dead animal. One woman provided John Green with an explanation for the stench: Bigfoot rolls around on rotting animal carcasses, just like her dog. "It will actually gag you, it is so disgusting," she says. The variety of Bigfoot found in Florida is so stinky that it has been nicknamed "Skunk Ape."

- Bigfoot is sometimes very noisy. It can slink around as quietly as a mouse when it wants to, but it also can make quite a racket when it is in the mood. The sounds it makes have been described as sounding like whoops, moans, grunts, a squealing pig, or a screaming woman. According to one report, Bigfoot screams "like a smashed cat." In addition to vocal sounds, it sometimes beats its chest, gorilla-style, or whistles. In fact, whistling is one of the most frequently reported Bigfoot sounds.

- Bigfoot has been spotted swimming underwater, kicking its legs like a frog and holding its arms out in front of its head. These sightings are very interesting because they fit with a few reports that claim the beast looked like it was covered with moss and slime. Perhaps people who made those reports saw a Bigfoot that had just crawled out of a pond or swamp.

- Bigfoot is a fast runner. Several people have claimed that a Bigfoot either chased them in their car or playfully ran alongside them as they tried to speed away from it. One man in New Mexico clocked a Bigfoot at 45 miles per hour (72 kilometers per hour). A hairy, 10-foot-tall (3-meter-tall) "Booger Man" from the Midwest chased a car going 60 mph (96 kph). And one time, a 6-foot-tall (3-meter-tall) Bigfoot with red eyes chased a car going 70 mph (112 kph) for a mile. But the champion was a skunk ape that ran beside a car zipping down a Florida highway at 80 mph (128 kph). To compare, the fastest known land animal, the cheetah, runs at no more than 60 mph (96 kph). That skunk ape would have left a sprinting cheetah in its dust!

To review: Bigfoot walks on two feet, stands as high as 10 feet tall (3 m), and weighs up to 1,000 pounds (455 kilograms). It has feet as big as 24 inches long (61 cm) and 12 inches wide (30 cm), with three, four, or five toes on each foot. Bigfoot is almost totally covered with white, red-brown, brown, or black hair, and has beady eyes that glow in the dark like colored lightbulbs. Finally, Bigfoot sometimes stinks like a rotten piece of roadkill, squeals like a pig, likes to whistle, swims like a frog, and can outrun any other animal on the face of the Earth.

And yet, this bear-sized beast has avoided being caught, trapped, killed, or even clearly photographed by humans ever since it was first observed hundreds, if not thousands, of years ago. Not even one bone from a dead Bigfoot has ever been found. It is no wonder that so many **skeptics**, including a lot of scientists, think Bigfoot is nothing more than a figment of the imagination.

Many cryptozoologists think differently, however, because there are still some pretty good arguments that suggest that Bigfoot may indeed exist.

A Step Back in Time

Some of the earliest evidence supporting the existence of Bigfoot is more than a thousand years old. Sometime between the years A.D. 700 and 1000, the ancient epic poem *Beowulf* was written. No one knows who wrote it, or exactly when or where it was written.

Many people know about the legendary Scandinavian warrior in the story, because *Beowulf* is often assigned reading in high school English class. What many people don't know, however, is that Beowulf's enemy, the powerful monster Grendel, in some ways resembles that hairy monster of modern times, Bigfoot. Note the similarities:

> Out from the marsh, from the foot of misty Hills and bogs . . . Grendel came . . . He moved quickly through the cloudy night, Up from his swampland, sliding silently . . . his eyes Gleamed in the darkness, burned with a gruesome Light.

Grendel hung out near water, just like Bigfoot. He was fast on his feet, just like Bigfoot. He was nocturnal, just like Bigfoot (most Bigfoot sightings are at night). His eyes glowed, just like Bigfoot's eyes. Ancient European **folklore** often includes stories about hairy "wild men" of the forest. Some people note that folklore often has a grain of truth behind it, and they believe that the author of *Beowulf* might have based Grendel on real creatures living in the ancient forests of Scandinavia.

At about the same time that *Beowulf* was written, Vikings led by Leif Ericson made their way to the east coast of North America. It was there that they reportedly encountered ugly, hairy beings that they called *skellrings*. Some people think the skellrings might actually have been Bigfoot. It is possible, however, that Native Americans wearing large animal skins fooled the Viking observers.

Sasquatch

Native Americans themselves have a long history of dealings with strange, hairy, humanlike creatures of the forest, especially in the Pacific Northwest. The folklore of several tribes from British Columbia, Canada, and the states of Washington, Oregon, and California is rich with tales of these beasts. The creatures described in this folklore often have supernatural powers, such as the ability to hypnotize other animals. These creatures are known by various names, including *Sésquac* and *Sasehavas*. The Canadian journalist J. W. Burns invented the familiar term *Sasquatch* from those names in the 1920s.

Another hairy beast went by the name of Seeahtlks, which sounds very much like Seathl, the name of a famous chief of the Suquamish Indian tribe. Although the city of Seattle, Washington, is named after chief Seathl, the similarity between the names Seeahtlks and Seathl has led at least one Bigfoot hunter, biologist Robert Pyle, to suspect that the name Seattle honors both the hairy man-beast and the Indian chief.

Ancient Native American artwork contains paintings and carvings showing apelike creatures. This is curious, because there are no known apes in North America, except, of course, in zoos. More than one old totem pole contains the carved image of a hairy beast known as Dzonoqua, whose ape face poses with its lips squeezed together, as if it is whistling. Bigfoot experts point to such artwork as evidence that Bigfoot really exists. They ask how else the native peoples could have come up with the idea for a whistling Sasquatch.

The library at Washington State University possesses a letter written in 1840 by Elkanah Walker, a missionary stationed in northern Washington. In this letter, Walker retells a story he heard while living with the Spokane tribe. The Spokane talked about a race of powerful, smelly giants who left footprints 1.5 feet (0.5 m) long. These giants were said to sneak into settlements at night in order to kidnap people and steal salmon from their fishing nets. Again, researchers ask, if Bigfoot doesn't exist, how did the Spokane come up with the idea for a smelly, big-footed Sasquatch?

Things get really interesting at the start of the twentieth century. By the early 1900s, many people were traveling, living, and working in the mountains of the American Northwest. Crews were busy building roads up into the Cascade Mountains so that logging crews could reach timber-rich forests. Miners were staking claims all over the land, searching for gold and other minerals. Woodsmen were out and about hunting bear and trapping beaver. Not surprisingly, some of these people had some exciting experiences as they invaded the land of the Sasquatch.

Kidnapped!

The year 1924 was a big one in the history of Bigfoot sightings. Not only was it the year of the Ape Canyon incident, but it was also the year that logger Albert Ostman claimed he was kidnapped and held prisoner by a whole family of Sasquatch. His story joins the legend of Ape Canyon as one of the all-time favorites of Bigfoot lore.

That summer, Ostman had taken time off from his lumberjack job. He decided to vacation in the mountains along the coast of British Columbia, Canada, where he intended to search for gold. He had heard stories about the Sasquatch tribe, a group of giant, hairy humans living in those mountains. He had even heard a rumor that a gold miner who had disappeared a while back might have been killed by these giants. Ostman didn't believe any of the stories, so off he went on his mountain trek without a worry.

On the third night of his trip, however, Ostman was rudely awakened. Someone picked up his sleeping bag—with him still in it—and walked off with it. For three hours, Ostman was jostled and dragged along, scrunched up into a helpless ball in the bottom of his sleeping bag. He was unable to move his arms to reach his knife or rifle in order to fight his kidnapper or try to escape. Finally, just before dawn, Ostman's cramped and crazy journey ended when the kidnapper dumped the sleeping bag on the ground. The bewildered lumberjack crawled out of the bag, still not sure what was going on. In the gradually brightening light of dawn, Ostman was finally able to get a look at his captors. They were a group of four hairy, giant people: an old man, an old woman, a boy, and a girl.

The Sasquatch tribe really did exist! And they really were giants. The old man, the biggest of the group, was 8 feet tall (2.5 m) and very muscular. Even the boy was huge, at 7 feet tall (a bit over 2 meters) and about 300 pounds (136 kg).

Ostman was allowed to roam around the Sasquatch homestead. The area included a place for sleeping that was carpeted with moss and contained what looked like blankets made of woven strips of tree bark stuffed with moss.

Unfortunately for him, however, Ostman was not allowed to escape. He didn't want to use his rifle to fight his way out. He thought these hairy giants were really people, and he didn't want to shoot another person if he didn't have to. Besides, Ostman wasn't sure if his small rifle would be much good against these giants. He was certain, though, that they would get very angry if he did shoot at them. The consequences of that might not be very pleasant!

Ostman bided his time and watched his captors. He tried to befriend the boy and girl, and even shared tobacco from the snuff box he had stashed in his bag. Finally, on the sixth day, the old man himself gave Ostman the opening he was looking for. When Ostman pulled out his tobacco box, the old man came over, grabbed the box, and ate all the tobacco in one big gulp. Not surprisingly, the old man soon became extremely ill and ran down the hill to get a drink of water from the creek below. Ostman quickly gathered all his belongings and made a run for it, shooting a warning shot at the old woman to keep her and the others from following him. The relieved Ostman made good his escape and eventually made his way back to civilization.

To Tell the Truth

Was Albert Ostman really kidnapped by a Sasquatch? Was he really held prisoner by a Sasquatch family, a group of hairy giants who made blankets out of bark and moss, for nearly a week?

According to John Green, "The story does have at least two things very much wrong with it." First, the locations where Ostman claimed he started and ended his adventure were far apart and separated by mountains. The Sasquatch would have had to haul Ostman across a jagged mountain range for close to 50 miles (80 km) during that three-hour trip. That's almost 17 mph (27 kph) right through the rugged up-and-down forested slopes, with no rest stops along the way.

The second thing that bothered Green was the way Ostman described his captors. He referred to them as people—monstrously huge, hairy, naked people who lived and acted like members of a human family. There was a father who was obviously the boss. There was a mother and a son, who were in charge of gathering food (grass, twigs, and other plant material), and there was a gentle daughter. The Sasquatch family members even talked to each other in a weird, chattery language. The boy and girl, typical of human children, liked to play. One of the boy's favorite activities was to sit down, grab his feet in his hands, and bounce along on the ground until he tipped over. Ostman said the boy could sometimes go 20 feet (6 m) before he lost his balance. Ostman actually thought he could coax the girl to follow him back to civilization, but he figured he might need to house her in a cage.

When Green compared Ostman's story to the hundreds of others he collected, he noted that the behavior of Ostman's Sasquatch family was much more humanlike than the behavior of the apelike creatures described by everyone else. As a result, he had a hard time believing Ostman's account.

"In fact," he wrote, "if anyone came along with such a story today, I wouldn't pay any attention to him."

The simplest explanation for Albert Ostman's description of his captors is that he based it not on his own experience, but on stories told by fellow loggers and miners—stories based on Indian legends about the mysterious, hairy giants of the Sasquatch tribe. If this explanation is correct, then that would imply that Ostman made up the whole kidnapping story.

This argument is strengthened by the fact that Ostman provided so much detail in his story. For example, he recalled that he had six rifle bullets left, and that it was precisely 4:25 A.M. when he and his kidnapper arrived at the Sasquatch homestead. If Ostman had told his story as soon as he escaped and returned to civilization, such detail would be expected. But Ostman didn't tell his story right away. Instead, he waited—for 33 years. He didn't tell his story until 1957, after another Bigfoot story made a big splash in all the local newspapers. Some Bigfoot hunters feel that Ostman's incredibly detailed recollection of something that happened so many years ago smells of a hoax.

But some Bigfoot experts disagree. They think the incredible detail contained in Ostman's story makes it all the more reliable. As one famous Bigfoot researcher, Peter Byrne, put it, "to my way of thinking, the more detail there is, the more believable the story is." Still, even Byrne is unable to accept Ostman's story without more evidence, such as the capture of a real Sasquatch that looks like the "people" Ostman described.

When all these pieces are put together, Albert Ostman's story doesn't seem to hold much water. Many modern researchers of Bigfoot think Ostman's story was just a tall tale, a chance for an unknown logger to have his moment in the spotlight.

Where Is the Evidence?

Albert Ostman did not bring back any evidence to back up his story. Just think how much more believable his tale would have been if he had brought back some Sasquatch hair or a chunk of fingernail (he described the male Sasquatch's nails as looking like chisels). Imagine if he had smuggled away a piece of one of the bark blankets, or some other **artifact**. Without hard evidence to back up his story, Ostman had little proof that what he says happened actually happened. It may be entertaining, but it does not provide anything that scientists can study and evaluate.

That's the problem with most eyewitness accounts of Bigfoot encounters, including famous ones like Ostman's story and the legend of Ape Canyon, as well as the hundreds of other accounts that never became newspaper headlines. Without any hard evidence for Bigfoot researchers to examine, it's impossible to determine whether such stories are legitimate, whether they are honest cases of mistaken identity (mistakes made by people who thought they saw Bigfoot but really did not), or whether they are outright hoaxes. In the case of Bigfoot, hoaxes and mistaken identities are all over the place.

Many people have made their own fake Bigfoot feet, strapped them onto their boot bottoms, tromped around at night in the snow or dirt, and convinced others that Bigfoot had been there. Many supposed eyewitness sightings of Bigfoot have turned out to be bears or tree stumps. This happens most often in low-light conditions such as deep forest shadows, fog, heavy rain, or the dark of night. In such a spooky environment, even a dark boulder might look like a squatting Sasquatch to a person with an overactive imagination. There's no telling how many people have driven down a road through the deep woods at night and mistaken the shining eyes of a big owl, perched atop a jagged old tree stump, for the glowing eyeballs of a 10-foot-tall Sasquatch.

Fortunately, some sightings of Bigfoot and/or their tracks provide enough solid evidence to allow Bigfoot researchers to do scientific examinations. Then they can determine whether the sightings might be legitimate. Some of these accounts are just as bizarre as the stories of Ape Canyon and Albert Ostman. Let's take a closer look at these interesting cases and see what they have to offer.

BIGFOOT BECOMES FAMOUS

𝒥 n August 1958, workers from a road construction crew in northwestern California discovered trails of footprints. Every morning, they found new tracks of 16-inch-long (41 cm) humanlike footprints all over their work site overlooking the rugged mountain valley of Bluff Creek. Finally, one of the workers, a bulldozer operator named Jerry Crew, decided to make a plaster **cast** of one of the footprints. He then took the cast to the local newspaper, where a reporter interviewed him and took a picture of Crew holding the amazing footprint cast in his lap. Crew's story and photo spread like wildfire, leaping from newspaper to newspaper, all across the United States. Within days, Americans everywhere had been introduced to the footprint of the giant man-beast from Bluff Creek. People familiar with Indian legends recognized the creature as Sasquatch, but the rest of the country was introduced to the beast by a different name, one coined by the Bluff Creek road crew. That name has stuck ever since: *Bigfoot*.

Were those footprints real, or were they a hoax? That's a good question. As it turns out, Ray Wallace, the person in charge of building the Bluff Creek road, was known as a big-time practical joker. Similar footprints had appeared earlier that year at another one of Wallace's road construction sites. That certainly suggests that Wallace had something to do with the Bluff Creek prints. He had quite an imagination. He owned a collection of smooth, round rocks that he claimed Bigfoot used to kill deer and other animal prey. He claimed he had actual Bigfoot hair samples and Bigfoot photos. He claimed to have tossed apple treats to Bigfoot from his truck. He even claimed that he had once managed to capture a live Bigfoot, although he never did show it to anybody.

Wallace also gave other hints to suggest that it was all a joke. He took part in a lengthy interview with scientist Robert Pyle several years after the Bluff Creek incident. At the end of that interview, Wallace said, with a wink and a smile, "Don't waste your time looking for Bigfoot."

It is likely that Ray Wallace was the Bluff Creek Bigfoot, but that doesn't mean that all Bigfoot footprints are fakes. In fact, some Bigfoot researchers who examined the Bluff Creek prints thought that there might be some real Bigfoot prints mixed in with Wallace's fakes. Sometimes it is hard to detect a fake, especially if there is only one print to examine. But if there is a trail of several prints, that makes it a lot easier. The prints left by a person clomping around in wooden Bigfoot feet all look alike. Each left footprint looks exactly like all the other left footprints, and each right footprint looks exactly like all the other right footprints. Together, they make a bunch of identical cookie-cutter patterns.

On the other hand, footprints made by real feet aren't all the same. A person's footprint trail on a wet beach will show slightly different foot shapes with each step. For example, the outline of the sole changes a little. Sometimes the toes line up a little bit differently because the person was leaning a bit this way or that way, or speeding up or slowing down. Also, real feet are flexible. They wrap or bend around small stones or bits of wood sticking out of the sand. Fake wooden feet are too hard and stiff to wrap around such objects. They just teeter-totter over the top of them. If the toes leave behind any prints at all, they line up like predictable cookie-cutter prints.

Some Bigfoot researchers who have examined casts of the Bluff Creek footprints claim that some of the prints do indeed show slight differences in foot shape and toe position. Two of those prints are particularly interesting. According to researcher Dr. Jeff Meldrum, one of the prints appears to be slightly deformed by a twig on which the print-maker (whether man or beast) stepped. Also, Jerry Crew's famous footprint cast shows a slight dent along the inside edge, possibly the result of stepping against the side of a small rock.

And there's more: The step length (the distance from left footprint to right footprint) of the Bluff Creek tracks is nearly 5 feet (1.5 m). For a giant creature, that would be no problem. An average-sized human, however, has a step length much less than half that long. A human would need to take a big lunge forward with each step in order to create a step length of 5 feet. This would be a mighty challenge for a practical joker wearing big wooden feet strapped to his boots and climbing up and down rugged slopes covered with twigs and rocks.

Still, a clever, crafty prankster can fake even these seemingly legitimate footprints and tracks. All that a person needs is a fake foot that is more flexible than wood.

INTRODUCING RUBBERFOOT

It is easy to make really **authentic**-looking Bigfoot tracks, according to Bigfoot researcher Ron Baird of the Museum of Natural History at Princeton University. The trick is to use fake feet made from a material that is softer and more bendable than wood. The best material for this is rubber.

Bigfoot feet made of rubber can be carefully tapped down into soft soil with a mallet and stake. Different parts of the flexible foot will sink deeper into the soil than other parts. By varying the depth of different areas of the rubber foot from one print to the next, the appearance of identical

A resident of Vancouver, Washington, holds two wooden feet that he claims were used to make Bigfoot prints. Each wooden foot has a strap that allows it to be worn like a sandal.

Dr. Jeff Meldrum prepares a Bigfoot cast in his lab at Idaho State University. Meldrum is a professor of anatomy at the school. He is considered the world's foremost Bigfoot researcher and has spent more than 30 years studying the elusive creature.

cookie-cutter prints can be avoided. Also, the rubber will flex a bit if the foot is pressed down over a protruding stick or stone, making a print that seems even more real. By spacing these realistic prints far enough apart, super-long step lengths can be produced. To hide their own tracks, people making fake Bigfoot trails cover their own feet in sacks filled with leaves or some other fluffy material. This creates a soft cushion as they walk along, so that they don't leave their own telltale human prints alongside the Bigfoot prints. The result: an authentic-looking Bigfoot trail.

Many fake Bigfoot prints sink deep into the ground, sometimes to a depth of 1 to 2 inches (2.5 to 5 cm). These prints are designed to seem like the animal that made them

LET'S GET TECHNICAL: HOW TO MAKE A RUBBER BIGFOOT CAST

Rubber Bigfoot feet are more realistic than wooden ones, but the foot-making process is much more complicated than simply whittling a block of wood.

The first step in the process involves making a **mold** of a human footprint by stepping into a shallow pan or tray containing a wet, cementlike substance called plaster of Paris. Once the plaster has started to harden, the person moves his or her foot, leaving behind a detailed footprint mold. When the plaster has finished drying and hardening, the footprint mold is then painted with a few thin layers of liquid latex rubber. When the latex cast has dried, it can be peeled off the plaster mold.

And now for the fun part: The person making the fake foot applies special oil to the latex cast. This causes the rubber to swell and expand by up to 50%. For example, a cast of a human foot that is 10 inches weighed several hundred pounds. It is actually fairly easy to fake this. Anyone who has ever played around in mud puddles may already know how to do it. The wetter and deeper the mud, the farther a foot sinks into it. A practical joker using a hammer, stake, and fake foot can make an inch-deep Bigfoot print in a sloppy mud puddle. It would be much harder to press the foot down this deep into hard-packed dirt. If there are no mud puddles to be found, a prankster could bring along a bucket or two of water to gently but thoroughly soak a small patch of dry ground. He or she would then press a fake footprint into the softened soil. Once the soil dried, it would be impossible to tell that it had been a lot softer when the deep print was made. Then it would certainly seem like

long (25 cm) will grow to a length of 15 inches (38 cm). This size is quite appropriate for a medium-sized Sasquatch. Since the amount that latex expands depends on how much oil is applied, it's actually possible to change the shape of the cast by treating some areas with more oil and others with less. What started out as a cast of a smaller, narrower, human foot can be changed into a huge, fat, flat-footed Sasquatch foot.

The latex cast is too flimsy to use for making footprints itself, but it can be used to make a second plaster mold, which can then be used to make a thicker cast of much sturdier silicone rubber. A cast made from silicone is flexible, somewhat like the sole of a real foot. It is perfect for making realistic Bigfoot prints.

Serious jokesters remember to make casts of both the left and the right foot. Some people have made Bigfoot trails that are less than convincing, made up of all left-footed or all right-footed prints.

only a half-ton Sasquatch could have made that inch-deep footprint in hard dirt.

It is clear that people can make very realistic fake Bigfoot footprints. Still, there is one feature found on several Bigfoot print casts that has caught the attention of many Bigfoot researchers. Some casts show what look just like **dermatoglyphs**. Dermatoglyphs are complex patterns of tiny ridges and valleys that occur on the fingers, palms, feet, and toes of primates—monkeys, apes, and their relatives, including humans. The lines in a person's fingerprints are due to dermatoglyphs.

The fine detail of the dermatoglyphs on Bigfoot print casts suggests that they are real primate prints. In fact, many Bigfoot researchers believe dermatoglyphs to be the strongest of all the footprint evidence in favor of the existence of Bigfoot. One fingerprint expert, a police officer named Jimmy Chilcutt, studied many Bigfoot print casts. He was so impressed by some of the dermatoglyphs he saw that he risked his own good reputation among his fellow forensics experts. He announced in 2002 in a documentary video (*Sasquatch: Legend Meets Science*) that those dermatoglyphs were proof that a huge, unknown species of primate lives in the Pacific Northwest.

Yet, the skeptics still are not convinced. One such doubter, artist Matt Crowley, performed an extensive series of experiments testing different types of cast-making materials (such as plaster of Paris) and different types of soil, including the very fine, powdery soil typical of Bluff Creek and other areas where footprints with dermatoglyphs have been found. Using this type of soil, Crowley was able to make casts that contained ridges that looked just like dermatoglyphs—even though the fine-grained, smooth-surfaced soil molds he made were totally ridge-free.

This experiment showed that so-called dermatoglyph ridges were nothing more than ridges that grew on the

This close-up image shows a Bigfoot cast with ridges. Some experts argue that the ridges are dermatoglyphs, while others believe they are desiccation ridges created during the casting process.

surface of the plaster during the cast-making process. These fingerprintlike lines are known as *desiccation ridges*. They form when dry underlying soil soaks up water and dries out the bottom surface of the freshly poured casting material as it slowly spreads out over the surface of the footprint mold. In this case, the evidence provided by supposed dermatoglyphs is not the result of a deliberate hoax. It's simply a result of the footprint casting process.

JUST THE BEGINNING

It doesn't matter much anymore whether or not Ray Wallace was the only species of bipedal primate stomping around the Bluff Creek construction site back in 1958. The last of the Bluff Creek prints is long gone. Furthermore, Wallace's reputation as a dedicated Bigfoot prankster has tarnished the whole Bluff Creek incident. Because of this, many skeptical Bigfoot researchers don't believe any of those old prints or their casts are very good evidence for the existence of Bigfoot.

Yet, Bluff Creek was just the beginning. Once Americans became aware of the possible existence of Bigfoot, some people started looking for the creature. Many of them were successful. There are many sightings of Bigfoot and Bigfoot **spoor**—footprints, trails, or other evidence—compared to the number of sightings of lesser-known cryptids. Four of these Bigfoot sightings and spoor stand out above the rest. The evidence supporting those four is spectacular and seemingly impossible to fake or mistake—at least at first glance.

One such sighting, the most famous one of all, occurred only a few miles from the stretch of Bluff Creek where Ray Wallace made his mark in the history of Bigfoot lore. This Bigfoot sighting raised such a ruckus that it quickly turned a little-known Bigfoot hunter from the state of Washington into a national celebrity. His name? Roger Patterson.

CAPTURING BIGFOOT . . . ON FILM

*R*oger Patterson was an ex-rodeo rider. He was also a Bigfoot fanatic. He was obsessed with the huge creature and hunted down every story, every fact, and every detail about Bigfoot that he could find. He even wrote a book on the subject titled, *Do Abominable Snowmen of America Really Exist?*

Patterson's book was published in 1966, and in it he presented many attention-grabbing newspaper stories about Bigfoot. More than anything else, Patterson wanted to prove to the world that Sasquatch really existed. That's exactly what he did . . . or, at least, that's what he claimed he did.

CASE #1: THE PATTERSON FILM

The year after his book was published, Patterson and his friend Bob Gimlin went hunting for Bigfoot—with a movie camera, not a gun. (Gimlin did bring along his rifle, though, just in case they met up with a Bigfoot with a bad attitude.) The two men, being experienced horsemen, decided to track Bigfoot on horseback. Although they both lived in Washington, they decided to conduct their Sasquatch search in northwest California because so many sightings of Bigfoot prints had been reported there.

After loading up Gimlin's truck and horse trailer with supplies and three horses—two riding horses and a packhorse to carry food and camping equipment—the two men drove to Bluff Creek. They made their way to a spot not too far from the old Ray Wallace road construction site. After only a few days of searching for Sasquatch spoor, Patterson and Gimlin made the discovery of a lifetime.

According to Patterson, as he and Gimlin quietly made their way around a big tangle of dead tree branches and roots

THE ABOMINABLE SNOWMAN

Something that is **abominable** is disgusting and hateful. The term "abominable snowman" dates back to the 1920s. It was the name given by journalist Henry Newman to a bearlike or apelike creature that was said by natives of Tibet to inhabit the Himalaya mountain range. This rather insulting term is actually believed to be a mistranslation by Newman of the Tibetan name for the beast, which means "wild man of the snows"—a much less colorful, but perhaps more accurate, name. This creature is also known as the Yeti.

stuck in the nearly dry creek bed, they came upon a Bigfoot squatting along the edge of the creek, barely 60 feet (18 m) away. It seemed that the Bigfoot hadn't heard the muffled clumping of the horses' hooves approaching along the soft streambed. The creature was startled by their sudden appearance and quickly stood up and started to walk away.

The beast's sudden movement spooked the horses, and Patterson's horse reared up, slipped, and fell over, throwing Patterson to the ground. He quickly got up, grabbed his movie camera, and started filming the retreating Bigfoot. Patterson chased the animal, filming it as he ran, until at one point the creature paused, turned around, and glared right at him. Seeing that ominous stare, Patterson stopped dead in his tracks, but he kept filming the Bigfoot after it turned back around and continued walking toward the nearby woods.

The movie camera quickly ran out of film, because Patterson had already used up most of it filming other subjects. The Bigfoot footage he got—barely a minute's worth—was destined to turn the world of cryptozoology upside down. The star of the film was thought to be female since it had large, furry breasts. "She" was dubbed "Patty." The film was an instant sensation, and Patterson himself became an instant celebrity as his film appeared on TV screens across the country. From the moment Patterson went public with his movie, the film was also surrounded by a controversy that has yet to be resolved. Was "Patty" a real animal, or was she a person in an ape costume? Many Bigfoot researchers think Patty was the real deal, but there is a fair amount of evidence that suggests that "she" was a hoax.

Putting Patty to the Test

Probably the most controversial part of the Patterson film was the way Patty walked. She didn't walk like a human. Patty walked hunched over, and her knees were always slightly bent as she quickly and smoothly strode along, swinging her arms back and forth as she went. Many Bigfoot researchers think that no person, with or without a monkey suit, could walk that way without looking awkward and clumsy. But Patty made it look easy—perhaps too easy. Smithsonian Institution anthropologist John Napier viewed the Patterson film and remarked that Patty's smooth "body movements and the swing of the arms were to my mind grossly exaggerated . . . the walk was 'self-conscious.'" It was as if Patty wanted to make sure that anyone watching her was convinced that she was walking like an ape-woman, not a human.

Famous Bigfoot researcher Grover Krantz, an anthropologist at Washington State University, had a different opinion. Krantz, who was one of the first scientists to stick his neck out and admit to skeptical colleagues that he thought Bigfoot might really exist, believed Patty was a real Sasquatch. He said her gait (the way she walked) was too awkward for a person to be able to imitate it.

Then, anthropologist David Daegling and his colleague Daniel Schmitt, an expert in human motion, analyzed Patty's walk. They determined that it could be copied by walking with a compliant gait. When walking this way, a person's knees are always bent and the body doesn't move up and down the way it does during normal walking. It's easy, though tiring, to take quick, long steps when walking with a compliant gait. This is significant because Patty walked at a rapid pace along the Bluff Creek riverbed and left footprints 41 inches (76 cm) apart. To get an entertaining idea of what a human walking with a compliant gait looks like, check out some of the old Marx Brothers movies from the 1920s and 1930s, such as *Duck Soup*. Groucho Marx often clowned around by walking with a goofy compliant gait—what Daegling refers to as the "Groucho walk"—as he strode in front of the camera.

The importance of Daegling and Schmitt's study is that it shows that humans can indeed walk the way Patty did

Bigfoot hunter Roger Patterson filmed this Bigfoot in 1967. Many Bigfooters believe this film is legitimate, but many others insist it is a hoax.

Grover Krantz holds up a footprint cast taken after a Sasquatch sighting. Krantz was a respected anthropologist at Washington State University and one of the leading authorities on Bigfoot, until he passed away in 2002.

in Roger Patterson's film. Even Dr. Jeff Meldrum, who is more accepting of the possibility that Bigfoot really exists, acknowledges the significance of the two researchers' study. But Meldrum points out that there's more to Patty's walk than the way she moved. The speed at which she moved also needs to be considered, because animals, including people, walk differently at different speeds. For example, people take longer steps and swing their arms more when walking fast than when walking slowly. If Patty's pace could be determined from the movie clip, it might be possible to determine if a person in a costume would be physically able to perform that walk along the Bluff Creek streambed.

Normally, it's easy to determine how fast a person in a movie is walking: Find out how fast the movie camera was running (that is, how many individual frames of film were being exposed each second) when the person was filmed. For example, if the camera was running at 16 frames per second (fps) and 8 frames of film were used during each step the person took, then the person's walking speed must have been 2 steps per second:

$$\frac{1 \text{ step}}{8 \text{ frames}} \quad \text{x} \quad \frac{16 \text{ frames}}{\text{second}} \quad = \quad \frac{2 \text{ steps}}{\text{second}}$$

Using this reasoning, it should be easy enough to figure out how fast Patty was walking in the Patterson film clip. Unfortunately, that's not the case, because Patterson claimed he couldn't recall whether the camera was running at 16 fps or 24 fps when he filmed Patty. That little detail is a key piece of the puzzle surrounding Patty's performance, according to Don Grieve, a British scientist who studied the film.

Grieve's analysis of the film shows that it took Patty between 22 and 23 frames of film to complete one full **walking cycle**—the combination of a left footstep plus a right footstep. If she was filmed at 24 fps, then a complete walking cycle took just slightly less than one second. If she was filmed at 16 fps, then one complete walking cycle took almost 1.5 seconds. According to Grieve, if Patty was filmed at 24 fps, then she was walking fairly quickly, and her walking style, complete with long steps and widely swinging arms, could be easily, naturally, and smoothly performed by a fast-walking person in a costume. On the other hand, if Patty was filmed at 16 fps, then her pace was much slower, and the person in the costume would have to pretend to be walking quickly while actually moving in slow motion.

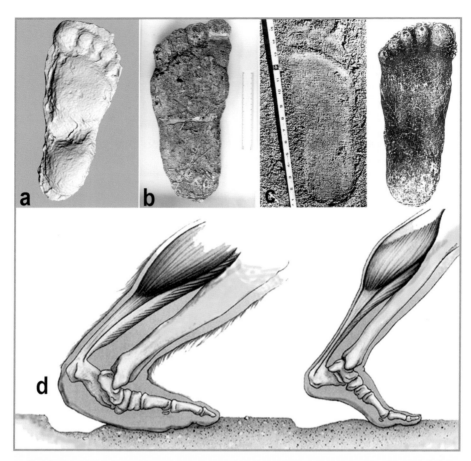

Footprint casts include: (a) a cast of a footprint left by the Bigfoot seen in the Patterson film; (b) a cast of a footprint found near Bluff Creek that was made four years before the Patterson film; and (c) a cast made from a footprint a few weeks after the Patterson film, and also found near Bluff Creek. Some experts believe that the footprints were left by the same Bigfoot. The bottom figure (d) shows the type of foot that may have created these prints (*left*), beside a human foot (*right*). Note that the foot at left has no arch and the skeletal structure is much different than that of the human foot. This model is the work of Bigfoot researcher Dr. Jeff Meldrum.

Grieve felt that a human walking in slow motion would have some difficulty maintaining his or her balance, and therefore would not be able to move as smoothly and naturally as Patty did. (You can easily demonstrate the effect of "slo-mo wobble" by pretending to run in slow motion. It's very difficult to keep your balance while slowly going through the motions of running.) Grieve concluded that the film was more likely shot at 24 fps than at 16 fps. If that was indeed the case—and we'll never know for sure—then Patty could easily have been a person in an ape suit.

An Inch Here, an Inch There

Another way to determine whether or not Patterson's Bigfoot was a fake is to see how the lengths of Patty's arms and legs compare to those of a human. To do this requires calculating the intermembral index (IM for short), a number that shows how long the arms are compared to the length of the legs. The formula for the IM is as follows:

$$\text{IM} = \frac{\text{Distance from the shoulder to the wrist}}{\text{Distance from the hip to the ankle}} \times 100$$

If the shoulder-to-wrist distance is the same as the hip-to-ankle distance (in other words, the arms and legs are the same length), the IM is equal to 100. If an animal's IM is less than 100, its arms are shorter than its legs, and if its IM is greater than 100, its arms are longer than its legs. Scientists have calculated IM values for all sorts of primates. People have an IM of about 70, which means that their arms are roughly 70% as long as their legs. The orangutan, which uses its long arms to swing from tree branch to tree branch, has

LET'S GET TECHNICAL: INTERMEMBRAL INDEX

*T*he intermembral index (IM) is a measure of the length of an animal's arms compared to the length of its legs. Arm length (the distance from the shoulder to the wrist) is calculated by adding together the lengths of the upper arm bone (the **humerus**) and the major forearm bone (the **radius**). The wrist and hand are not included. Similarly, leg length (the distance from the hip to the ankle) is calculated by adding the lengths of the upper leg bone (the **femur**) and the major lower leg bone (the **tibia**). The ankle and foot are not included. The IM is simply the value of the ratio of arm length to leg length, multiplied by 100.

The IM is a useful tool for studying ape biology. The IM of a particular species gives a good idea of how it gets around. For example, long-legged humans have an IM of 70 and tend to get around by walking on two feet. The orangutan, on the other hand, has an IM almost twice that value—134. Orangutans use their long arms to swing from tree branches. If humans had an IM of 134, their arms would be almost twice as long as normal. Gorillas have an IM of 120. Although they can walk on two feet for short distances, they are rather awkward at it. They are really designed to walk on all fours. Patty's IM was estimated to be 88. This means that, like humans, her legs were longer than her arms. Thus, it is not at all surprising that she walked fairly upright on two feet.

This silverback gorilla, like all gorillas, is more comfortable walking on all fours rather than walking on two feet.

an impressive IM of 134. That means that its arms are about 1.34 times longer than its legs.

What about Patty? Computer animator Reuben Steindorf carefully studied the way Patty's limbs moved up and down, back and forth, and pinpointed as accurately as he could the locations of all the arm and leg joints. This allowed him to estimate arm and leg lengths. It turns out that Patty had an IM of 88, a value quite a bit higher than the human IM of 70. This would seem to indicate that Patty couldn't be a person in a monkey suit. Her arms were just too long.

Skeptics have reason to question the accuracy of the IM calculated for Patty. It is extremely hard to pinpoint the exact location of any point of interest on Patty's body by just relying on the images in the Patterson film. Journalist John Green has studied that film as much as anybody. Even he had to admit that he tried to measure Patty's height many times, but he never came up with the exact same figure twice in a row. This is because the image of Patty on the film is so fuzzy. There are a number of reasons for this. First, Patty herself is furry and shaggy. Also, the movie camera shook as Patterson ran after the Bigfoot, blurring the image on the film. Furthermore, because she was off in the distance, Patty occupied only a tiny portion of each frame of the film. Any enlargements of the frames magnify Patty, but they also magnify the furriness and blurriness of all her features. This means that it is extremely difficult to locate the exact position of any point on Patty's body, whether it's the top of her skull or the location of her hip joint.

Also, Bigfoot journalist Greg Long, who interviewed countless people in his attempt to identify the person in the ape suit, located a man who claimed he made and then sold an ape suit to Roger Patterson—although he had no receipt to prove it—some time before the Bluff Creek movie was filmed. The costume maker, a man named Philip Morris, said he recognized the suit the moment he saw the Patterson film on TV. He did not make female gorilla costumes, though, and said Patty's breasts must have been "add-ons" installed by someone else. He guessed they could possibly be made using sand-filled balloons covered with bits of fur cut from an extra piece of costume fur that Patterson supposedly purchased along with the gorilla suit.

Morris explained to Long how he manufactured his gorilla costumes, and he explained how to make the costume's arms longer than its wearer's arms. This could be done by inserting sticklike extensions down into the sleeves, attaching the costume's black gorilla-hand gloves to the extensions, and then rolling the furry sleeves down to hide the sticks. The result? Extra-long arms.

Morris also explained that by inserting football shoulder pads underneath the costume fabric, the costume's shoulders could be raised above the wearer's shoulders, making the arms appear even longer. In addition, the seat of the pants portion of the costume hung just a little bit low, which made the wearer's legs appear shorter and more gorillalike. Therefore, by adding an inch or two here and there with shoulder pads and arm extensions, and subtracting a bit of leg length by lowering the seat of the pants, it would be possible to create a Bigfoot costume that had an IM value much larger than that of the human wearing it. In other words, Patty's high IM value may be simply due to the measure of a carefully crafted optical illusion.

Stacking the Evidence

When thinking about a subject as important and exciting as the possibility of a huge, undiscovered apelike creature, it's hard to maintain an open mind on the matter until all the facts are in. It's much easier to jump the gun and, based on the limited evidence at hand, form an opinion about the likelihood of Bigfoot's existence. It is easy to let eagerness influence the interpretation of the limited facts that do exist. This may result in a slanted or biased conclusion. Much Bigfoot evidence can easily be stacked one way or the other, supporting either the Sasquatch skeptic or the Bigfoot believer. Therefore, one of the biggest challenges facing Bigfoot researchers is to consider all the reasonable explanations for every piece of evidence—not just the ones that support a particular gut feeling.

This approach is especially important when the evidence is so unclear. That is the case with the Patterson film. Roger Patterson filmed his Bigfoot movie 40 years ago, and the skeptics and the believers are still arguing over whether a person in a costume could walk like Patty did. Each side promotes interpretations that support its own stance and downplays interpretations that support the opposing stance.

Patty's walk is just the tip of the iceberg. There are scores of details in the Patterson film that could be interpreted to support either skeptics or believers. Let's look at a few.

One of the most noticeable things about Patty is an unnatural-looking band of light that streaks across her dark face at eye level. A believer could claim that this streak is due either to sunlight reflecting on the animal's skin or to a light-damaged spot on the film. On the other hand, a skeptic could say that the band looks like a simple mask cutout for the eyes and nose of a human who appears to have light skin. The fact of the matter is that the image is just too blurry to tell.

Another notable feature about Patty is how muscular she looks, and how her muscles seem to ripple with power as she strides along the creek. A believer could claim that such massive, rippling muscles couldn't possibly be faked with a costume. A skeptic could claim that a Bigfoot costume could be made from fake fur attached to a snug-fitting leotard worn by a muscular, stocky human. Or, a skeptic might argue that the huge flexing muscles are just an optical illusion caused by rippling shadows in the costume's fur (after all, it was sunny the day Patty was filmed). Again, the image is just too blurry to tell.

There also appears to be an injury to Patty's right leg, above her knee. A bump is visible under the fur in several frames of the movie. It also looks as if Patty's right leg moves in a slightly abnormal fashion when she walks, possibly as a result of that injury. Then again, one could argue that the little bulge might simply be an imperfection or small tear in the material of a costume pant leg. The unusual leg movement might just be the way the jokester walked in the sand while wearing oversized, furry slipper-feet, which were part of the costume that Philip Morris claims he sold to Roger Patterson. Once again, the image is just too blurry to tell.

Speaking of Patty's feet, the soles of both are clearly seen in some frames of the movie. They stand out because their

ONE PHONY BIGFOOT

ournalist Greg Long believes he found the Bigfoot inside Roger Patterson's ape suit: a fellow named Bob Heironimus, one of Patterson's friends. After Heironimus confessed to Long that he was the man in the ape suit, he demonstrated his Bigfoot walk, wearing jeans, a jacket, and a baseball cap instead of an ape costume. Long couldn't believe how similar Heironimus's walk was to Patty's walk. He was a dead ringer for the female Bigfoot. Also, at slightly over 6 feet tall, he was just the right size. Wearing a football helmet—for a dome-head effect—decorated with fake fluffy fur, he would have been close to 6.5 feet tall (2 m), which is similar to Patty's approximated height. Of course, believers could still argue that just because Heironimus had the right height and build to play Patty, and that he claimed to have played Patty, doesn't mean he actually did.

very light color contrasts with Patty's dark, hairy legs. The interesting thing about the soles is that their shape doesn't match the shape of the footprints Patty supposedly left behind in the sand. In particular, the sole of the left foot looks oddly rectangular, with a sharply squared-off heel. The plaster cast that Patterson made of Patty's left footprint has a rounded heel. This might suggest that either Patty or her footprints—or both—are fakes. On the other hand, that squared-off look of the heel might simply be due to fur hanging over and covering up the rounded back edge of the heel. As is the case with the rest of this film's mysteries, the image is just too blurry to tell.

Finally, researchers debate the look of Patty's fur. It's the same all over, and that is very unlike real apes. Ape hair is often different on different parts of the animal's body. It may be thicker in one spot versus another, longer in one place, shorter in another, darker in one area, and lighter somewhere else. For example, the hair on the arms and legs of an ape is often longer than the hair on the body. Body hair on an ape may also be a little thin. Patty's hair, however, looks pretty much the same all over: The head, arms, legs, and body are all covered in what looks like the same glossy, dark brown fur.

A skeptic could claim that this is exactly what is expected from a gorilla costume made entirely from one type of furry fabric. A believer could counter by pointing out that since Patty is not one of those other apes, what applies to them doesn't necessarily apply to her. Furthermore, Bigfoot is usually found in colder climates, where thick fur all over the body might be expected.

As these examples show, the evidence from practically any detail in the Patterson film can be interpreted to defend either side of the controversy. In fact, skeptics and believers have used nearly all of the above arguments to forcefully promote their own side. This is all because none of the evidence is solid enough to have only one possible explanation.

Even the use of computer photo editing programs to improve or "sharpen" digital copies of individual frames from Patterson's film hasn't solved anything. Bigfoot believers claim that such improvements show details, such as Patty's teeth and a breast nipple, that couldn't be faked. Skeptics claim that such changes can make "something out of nothing"; that is, the photo editing process may create artifacts that were not present in the original movie frame.

A Script for Patty

There's still one more twist to the Patty story that deserves mention. While gathering Bigfoot newspaper articles for the book he published the year before he filmed Patty, Roger Patterson obtained some articles from John Green. One of those clippings reported a story told by a man named William Roe. He was an experienced outdoorsman, hunter, and trapper. One day, while out hiking in the wilds of British Columbia, Roe came upon a clearing in the brush and spotted what he thought was a grizzly bear behind a bush on the far side of the clearing. Rather than shoot it for its skin, Roe decided to sit back and watch the bear for a while. A few moments later, the animal stood up and walked into the clearing.

That's when Roe found out that it was no bear. It was a humanlike creature covered in brown fur, and stood 6 feet tall (2 m) and 3 feet wide (1 m). It had hairy breasts, so Roe figured it was a female. The creature was unaware that Roe was there. It wandered in his direction, squatted down next to a nearby bush, and began to nibble on leaves.

A short time later, the creature suddenly noticed Roe sitting there watching her. She quickly stood up and started to walk away, back toward where she had entered the clearing. Part of the way across the clearing, she paused and turned to look at him, as if to say she didn't want to have anything to do with him. Then she turned back and headed into the brush, where she tilted her head back and let loose with a high-pitched call before heading into the nearby woods.

Sound familiar? Except for a few details at the beginning and the end, Roe's story could easily have been the script for Roger Patterson's film. Could it be a coincidence?

MOVING ALONG

The evidence at this point in time casts a cloud of suspicion over the truthfulness of Roger Patterson's Bigfoot film. Many Bigfoot researchers are completely convinced that it is a hoax. Some others still believe Patty is, or at least might be, a real Bigfoot. Unfortunately, without concrete evidence (such as the actual costume), there's no absolute proof that the Patterson film is a hoax. The evidence is just too blurry to make a decision either way.

There are major drawbacks to analyzing evidence based only on photos and films. Researchers need an actual specimen to examine up close and personal. As luck would have it, within a year of Patty's appearance, two big-time cryptozoologists heard about a man who supposedly had found such a specimen. This man claimed he had the frozen corpse of a big, hairy brute that might be a real Bigfoot.

THE FROZEN CORPSE

*T*he Patterson film is the most famous Bigfoot story of all time, but the tale of the Minnesota Iceman is surely the most bizarre. It is a story of cryptid mystery that has never been topped, and it probably never will be. The person who played the hoax managed to fool two well-known cryptozoologists whom other researchers greatly admired. This person fooled them with the very clever use of one very simple object: an ice cube.

CASE #2: THE MINNESOTA ICEMAN

In the winter of 1968, barely 14 months after Roger Patterson filmed Patty, **zoologists** Ivan Sanderson and Bernard Heuvelmans traveled to visit Frank Hansen in frigid

Minnesota. Hansen was in charge of a most unusual carnival exhibit there: Within the protected walls of a special casket were the remains of a naked, hairy, humanlike beast, literally frozen in time. The hairy corpse was trapped within a huge block of ice that completely filled the casket.

Sanderson was a well-known author and Bigfoot expert, and Heuvelmans was the very founder of the science of cryptozoology. Together, the two men spent two days studying this Minnesota Iceman, taking notes and measurements, making drawings, and photographing the icy body. Even though they could only view the corpse through a thick layer of foggy, blurry ice, both men were able to see enough detail to be convinced that the Iceman was authentic. This impression was no doubt made stronger by the thick smell of rotting flesh sneaking out from one of the corners of the coffin.

Heuvelmans was so convinced that the Iceman was legit that he quickly published an article describing the creature, which he named *Homo pongoides*. The fact that Heuvelmans placed the Iceman in the same genus as humans (*Homo sapiens*) shows that he thought the Iceman was actually a close relative of our own species, not some sort of ape. Sanderson was equally excited about the hairy human Popsicle. He contacted primate expert John Napier, urging him to involve the world-famous Smithsonian Institution in the Iceman investigation. Napier convinced officials at the Smithsonian to approve the investigation. Before that could happen, though, a suspicious turn of events occurred that caused the Smithsonian to wisely back out of the investigation.

What happened to cause the Smithsonian to reverse gears? Just after the institution announced it would become involved in the study of the Iceman, Hansen announced that the original Iceman in the carnival was going to be replaced by a fake. The fake would be a model of the original. The original corpse—supposedly owned by a mysterious,

LET'S GET TECHNICAL: NAMING ANIMALS

*S*cientists classify each type of animal by giving it an official two-part Greek or Latin name. The first part is the animal's **genus** name, and the second part is its **species** name. A species is what we normally recognize as a particular kind of animal, such as a timber wolf or a snapping turtle. Closely related species are grouped together in the same genus. No two species in that genus are given the same species name, so each species' two-part name is unique. For instance, the timber wolf is *Canis lupus* and its relative the coyote is *Canis latrans*. This two-part naming system avoids the confusion that nicknames produce. For example, the timber wolf and the gray wolf are not different species; they are just different nicknames for *Canis lupus*.

anonymous businessman—was not going to be exhibited anymore. No one, not even scientists, would be able to access it.

This bit of news raised more than a few eyebrows at the Smithsonian. Hansen's story was certainly damaged by this announcement. It was damaged even further when Hansen changed his story about the origin of the corpse. He originally claimed that the Iceman was discovered floating in a block of sea ice off the coast of Siberia and was transported, still frozen, to the United States. Some time later, however, Hansen admitted that the whole Siberian ice cube story was just a tall tale he invented to go along with his carnival exhibit. The "true" story was that he actually shot and killed the Iceman in Minnesota one winter when it attacked him while he was out deer hunting. After the body froze in the frigid winter air, he transported it to a freezer and eventually "iced" it and put it on exhibit.

It didn't take long for Napier to suspect fraud. He was convinced that the Iceman was phony and that Hansen was suffering from a case of cold feet. Hansen knew that if the scientists from the Smithsonian got their hands on the corpse, they would quickly determine that it was a phony, and that would be the end of his sideshow attraction.

Napier became suspicious not only because of the strange turn of events, but also because careful study of the **anatomy** of the Iceman revealed details that just didn't make sense. For example, the feet had an awkward blend of human and ape characteristics and appeared to be made neither for walking on two feet nor for climbing trees. An analysis of the hands showed that they also had an unusual mix of ape and human features.

And what about that rotten smell coming out of the coffin? It was a very persuasive bit of "evidence" suggesting that the Iceman was indeed a real corpse. If the Iceman was a fake, then where did that smell come from? That special effect would actually be easy to produce. All it would take is a slab of rotting meat carefully hidden somewhere within the coffin—perhaps under the "corpse" or in a secret compartment within a coffin wall—to produce the desired aroma.

Not surprisingly, Napier concluded that the Iceman was the product of human imagination, not of nature. No wonder the Smithsonian backed out! Looking back, it's hard to believe that anyone took the Iceman seriously. How, then, did two experienced Bigfoot experts like Sanderson and Heuvelmans get caught by Hansen, hook, line, and sinker? They simply acted too quickly on their excitement. Instead of taking it slow, they let wishful thinking take control. They hoped that the Iceman was real, and that hope was enough to make them believe. They did not wait for the opportunity to thaw the Iceman and perform an actual hands-on examination of the body. Hansen surely would have denied them that opportunity, which would have made them immediately suspicious.

The saga of the Minnesota Iceman provides an important lesson to all eager cryptozoologists: Don't jump the gun or let wishful thinking cloud your judgment. A Bigfoot researcher's job is hard enough as it is. Being quick to make judgments makes that job harder.

CASE #3: CRIPPLE FOOT

Now it's time to look at the most twisted case in the history of Bigfoot investigations: the case of Cripple Foot. This incident took place outside the small mining town of Bossburg, Washington. It happened in the winter of 1969, less than a year after the meltdown of the Minnesota Iceman caper. (The late 1960s were busy times for Bigfoot researchers!)

One day, a curious set of what looked like Bigfoot footprints was discovered near the trash dump at the edge of town. The prints were huge, almost 18 inches long (46 cm). The left footprint looked like a typical Bigfoot print, but the right footprint was even more unusual. It was deformed. It was fatter than the left print, the toes were stubby and bent at odd angles, and the front of the foot was bent inward. It looked like the foot had been squeezed, squished, and twisted all at once. People who looked at this footprint figured the Bigfoot who made it must have had a deformed foot. They named the creature Cripple Foot.

Bigfoot researchers Ivan Marx, a hunting guide who had recently moved to Bossburg, and René Dahinden, formerly a farm worker from Switzerland, set about searching for more signs of Cripple Foot. They were soon rewarded with the discovery of a long trail of Cripple Foot tracks that seemed to wander aimlessly through the snow. There were more than 1,000 prints in all, leading this way and that, up hills and down, and even over a barbed wire fence more than 3 feet tall

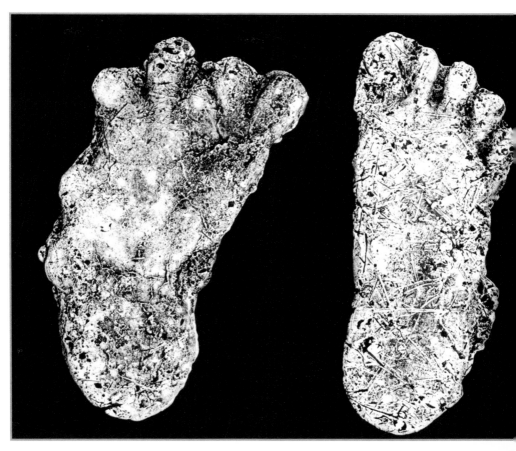

Two 17-inch casts of the Cripple Foot Sasquatch from Bossburg, Washington, were created in 1969.

(about 1 m). Cripple Foot seemed to have stepped over that fence as if it were no obstacle at all.

Dahinden made a plaster cast of Cripple Foot's right footprint. His cast intrigued cryptozoologists. Bigfoot expert Grover Krantz wasn't totally convinced that Bigfoot existed until he saw that Cripple Foot cast. His careful analysis of the print cast concluded that Cripple Foot likely suffered from a very real foot defect known as "clubfoot." Krantz concluded that no practical joker could possibly know enough about foot anatomy—especially foot defects—to be able to manufacture such a realistic clubfoot. Therefore, the footprint must

---

LET'S GET TECHNICAL: CLUBFOOT

Some children are born with a foot condition called *clubfoot*. It is believed to be hereditary, meaning that a child inherits it from his or her parents, grandparents, or other ancestors. It may also result from an injury to the foot or from a disease, such as polio.

There are several types of clubfoot. Each one is characterized by a different defect in the structure of the foot. According to anthropologist Dr. Jeff Meldrum, the type seen in Cripple Foot's footprint is called *metarsus adductus* (also known as *pes cavus*). In this form of clubfoot, there is an inward bending of the front half of the foot.

Infants born with clubfoot can be treated for the condition with special therapy in which the foot is carefully stretched out into a more normal position and then held in that position with a leg cast or brace. In severe cases, surgery may be required.

If Cripple Foot had been a real animal, it would have had a permanently deformed foot and would have spent its whole life hobbling around.

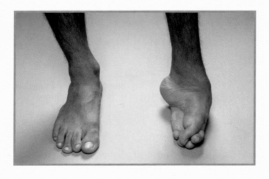

Clubfoot is a birth defect in which one or both feet are twisted out of position.

be authentic. And if the footprint was real, then Cripple Foot must be real. And that means . . . Bigfoot must really exist.

John Napier, who so quickly detected fraud in the Minnesota Iceman incident, agreed with Krantz in this case. In Napier's words: "It is very difficult to conceive of a hoaxer so subtle, so knowledgeable—and so sick—who would deliberately fake a footprint of this nature. I suppose it is possible, but it is so unlikely that I am prepared to discount it."

Would it really require an impossibly subtle, twisted, and knowledgeable mind to mastermind such a technically perfect hoax? Not necessarily. As David Daegling points out, many medical libraries possess illustrated anatomy books containing photographs of all sorts of feet: baby feet and adult feet, healthy feet and sick feet, normal feet and deformed feet—including those afflicted with clubfoot. It doesn't take the mind of a highly trained anthropologist like Krantz or Napier to find a photo of a clubfoot, make an enlargement of it, and use that as a model for making a fake Sasquatch foot. It just takes the mind of a clever, determined joker. And as this book has shown, there are plenty of those around.

The fact that cryptozoologists found and made a cast of the footprint of a seemingly crippled Bigfoot really doesn't prove anything. Cripple Foot's tracks do not prove anything, either. For one thing, more than one person noted that the tracks stayed conveniently close to a road, meaning that the joker did not need to venture far out into the wilderness. This also assured the joker that the prints would be quickly discovered.

Also, the starting and stopping points of Cripple Foot's trail were conveniently located on hard or rocky surfaces. That is just what is to be expected from a hoaxer using Cripple Foot boots. He or she could simply drive along the road to a suitable starting point, strap on fake Cripple Foot feet, take a stroll through a snowy field, and then head back

This still is from a film made by Ivan Marx in 1977. The film shows a Bigfootlike creature cavorting in the woods of northern California. As with Marx's film of Cripple Foot, experts who have examined the film believe that it is a fake and that the creature in the film is a man in an ape suit.

to the road. There, he or she could take off the fake feet and carry them back to the car, climb in, drive away, and have a good laugh, knowing that some hiker or truck driver would soon discover Cripple Foot's tracks.

That's not the only suspicious thing about Cripple Foot. The timing of the whole incident is most interesting. Cripple Foot's tracks showed up at the town dump right after Ivan Marx moved to Bossburg. It turns out that Marx was very much like Ray Wallace: full of crazy stories about everything from mountain lions to Bigfoot. He was quite likely a devoted hoaxer. Not only did he find Cripple Foot's tracks in the snow, he also managed to catch the creature on film. On film, Cripple Foot appeared to be about 9 feet tall (about 2.75 m). Reporter Peter Byrne later tracked down the site where the Cripple Foot movie was filmed. He was able to determine that the creature in Marx's film wasn't even 6 feet tall (2 m). Furthermore, Marx was seen buying furs in nearby Spokane, Washington, some time before he made the Cripple Foot film.

The Cripple Foot movie was an obvious hoax, which makes the Cripple Foot footprints more than a little suspect. In fact, journalist John Green, who got to know Marx pretty well while investigating Cripple Foot, was convinced that the entire Bossburg incident was one big practical joke concocted and carried out by Marx himself. Many Bigfoot hunters now agree. It is hard to take anyone's claims seriously once he or she has been exposed as a hoaxer.

So much for Cripple Foot. That's three cases down, one to go. The last one has the distinction of being the dirtiest Bigfoot case of all.

Case #4: Skookum

Skookum is the Chinook tribe's name for a powerful spirit that lives in the forest. Perhaps it is fitting that the last

Bigfoot story unfolds in a place called Skookum Meadows, in the heart of the Cascade Mountains. It was there that the Bigfoot Field Researchers Organization (BFRO), a group of dedicated Bigfoot researchers, decided to go Bigfoot hunting in September 2000. The team brought along a load of fancy equipment, such as heat detectors, night-vision cameras, and loudspeakers to broadcast human and animal sounds. This equipment was used to help attract and detect any Bigfoot in the area. The researchers decided to stake out a big mud puddle along the side of a private U.S. Forest Service road, in an area where strange noises had recently been heard during the night.

What turned out to be the most important tool the cryptozoologists brought along was also the simplest: bait, in the form of apples. The researchers figured that any hungry Bigfoot that came along would walk through the mud to reach the apples and leave behind nice, clear footprints in the process. So, late one night, they placed the apples in the middle of the puddle and then left the area.

When the investigators returned at dawn, an unusual sight greeted their hopeful eyes. The bait had obviously attracted something, because chunks of apples were strewn about the area. There was a weird pattern of bumps and dents and streaks in one section of the mud along the edge of the puddle. There were footprints of elk (a large type of deer) all over the place, but there were no clear Bigfoot prints anywhere. However, when the cryptozoologists took a close look at the weird marks in the mud, they came to a startling conclusion: A massive apelike beast had lain down in the mud.

The researchers saw what looked like heel prints (including the Achilles tendon, which connects to the heel and runs up the back of the ankle), knee prints, forearm prints, a hand print, a thigh print, and large buttock prints all within an area of about 17 square feet (1.6 square meters). There also were delicate, flowing, parallel patterns of lines in many of the prints, which could mean only one thing: hair. Whatever this creature was, it was hairy. It was also big: The size of the body part prints indicated that the creature was close to 9 feet tall (2.75 m). Furthermore, according to anthropologists who carefully studied the Skookum "body print," large buttocks and well-developed Achilles tendons are characteristic of one particular kind of animal: a primate that walks upright on its hind legs.

A huge, hairy primate that walks on its hind legs? In North America? There's only one creature that fits that description: Sasquatch. Studying the evidence like forensics detectives do at a crime scene, the BFRO researchers concluded that a large Bigfoot had approached the edge of the puddle, sat down, and leaned over on its left side. Then, propping itself up on its left elbow, it reached over the wettest part of the mud and grabbed the apples with its right hand.

This interpretation of the Skookum body print caught the attention of skeptics everywhere. They figured it made a lot more sense to conclude that an elk had made the mess in the mud and eaten the apples. There were elk hairs and hoof prints all around, but not even one clear Bigfoot footprint. It also seemed a bit silly to suggest that a Bigfoot would lie down in the muck and then grab the apples, instead of just walking over to the apples and picking them up.

Believers responded to these criticisms by pointing out that the mud wasn't all that mucky and wouldn't have stuck to a Bigfoot's hair. Furthermore, an elk would have left a different pattern of body part prints than the Skookum Bigfoot obviously did. They also argued that the dry ground surrounding the puddle was too hard for a Bigfoot to leave footprints. Also, the Bigfoot might have been trying to avoid leaving footprints, so that people couldn't follow it.

(A number of cryptozoologists believe that Bigfoot are smart and secretive enough to hide their spoor on purpose.)

The skeptics point out that this line of reasoning doesn't really make much sense, especially the part about the Bigfoot wanting to cover its tracks. After all, as journalist Benjamin Radford points out, if the Bigfoot didn't want anyone to know it was in the area, it surely would not have left behind a muddy body print. As far as the identity of the different body part prints is concerned, some researchers claim that the Bigfoot heel prints are actually elk knee prints. In fact, Bigfoot expert Anton Wroblewski photographed a resting elk "posing" in such a way that several of its body parts were in positions that closely matched the location of several features in the Skookum body print.

So, once again, some eager researchers' "solid evidence" has received a skeptical reception from many cryptozoologists after careful examination of all the details. Still, a lot of researchers are positive that Bigfoot really exists and that, sooner or later, someone is going to find hard evidence to prove it.

Not only that, many Sasquatch seekers are certain they know the exact identity of the beast they seek. They don't think it's an animal totally unknown to science. It's just an animal that hasn't been seen for a while—for about 200,000 years. Its fossil remains exist to prove that it once roamed the Earth and lived alongside ancient human ancestors. If these cryptozoologists are right, humans may someday find a long-lost neighbor, the largest ape that ever lived: the ape named Giganto.

GIGANTO

*I*magine an ape that stands 10 feet tall (3 m) and weighs as much as 1,200 pounds (545 kg), dwarfing the largest known ape, the gorilla. (A magnificent male silverback gorilla will tip the scales at 400 pounds, or 182 kg.) This giant ape's skull, from the bottom of the jawbone to the top of the sagittal crest, is 18 inches high (46 cm). That is almost twice as high as a gorilla's skull.

This animal's scientific name is *Gigantopithecus*, which means "gigantic ape." Such an ape has not been seen since "Giganto" reportedly became extinct 200,000 years ago. This was during the period in Earth's history known as the **Pleistocene Epoch**, which lasted from 1.8 million years ago to 11,000 years ago.

Compared to the gorilla, Giganto certainly is gigantic. But compared to Bigfoot, Giganto is a perfect fit. Many eyewitness reports of Bigfoot describe an apelike creature exactly Giganto's size. Not surprisingly, many Bigfoot experts believe this is no coincidence. They believe that Bigfoot is a living, breathing descendant of the giant ape of long ago. If they are right, Giganto is not extinct after all. This means cryptozoologists should be able to learn something about the biology of Bigfoot by studying Giganto's fossil remains. In fact, **paleontologists** and anthropologists have learned quite a bit from the few Giganto fossils they have found. What they have discovered may shed some light on the dark mystery surrounding Bigfoot.

NO BONES ABOUT IT

Unfortunately, scientists have yet to discover a complete Giganto fossil skeleton. They don't have any leg bones, arm bones, ribs, backbones, or skulls. All they have discovered so far are three jawbones and about a thousand teeth, all from fossil sites in China and Vietnam. From that extremely limited bunch of fossils, scientists have found out some very useful information about the life and times of the giant ape. Leading the way in the study of Giganto fossils is anthro- pologist Russell Ciochon. He has developed some interesting hypotheses about the natural history of this giant ape.

For example, much useful information has been obtained from studies of Giganto's teeth. By using a special microscope to obtain detailed close-up photographs of tooth surfaces, Ciochon and his colleagues have found important clues to Giganto's diet. The microscope images show tiny structures, **phytoliths**, stuck in the surface of the teeth. Phytoliths are tiny particles of a mineral called silica that is found in the cells of many types of plants. Since each type of plant produces its own shape of phytolith, Ciochon was able to determine the sources of the phytoliths found on the fossilized Giganto teeth. Most of the phytoliths were needle-shaped structures of the sort found in grasses such as bamboo, which was widespread where Giganto lived. The rest of the phytoliths

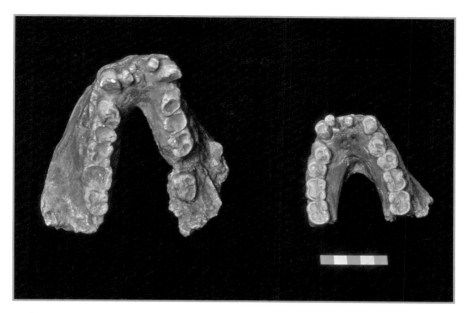

These two *Gigantopithecus* jawbones were discovered in China in 1955. Giganto's skull was nearly twice the size of a gorilla's and had a huge sagittal crest to support the ape's massive jaw muscles.

were cone-shaped structures found in the fruit of the durian or jackfruit tree. Based on this phytolith evidence, Ciochon proposed that Giganto was an **herbivore** (plant eater) whose diet was made up of a main course of bamboo, with an occasional side dish of fruit.

An herbivorous diet is also suggested by the structure of Giganto's teeth. The ape's front teeth were perfectly shaped for nipping pieces of vegetation such as tough blades of bamboo. The back teeth were sturdy and flat, perfect for grinding up plant material.

Furthermore, Giganto's jaw was extremely thick and massive, a condition commonly found among herbivores that eat lots of tough plant material. Such powerful jaws require extremely big, strong muscles. Ciochon reasoned

LET'S GET TECHNICAL: TYPES OF TEETH

Examination of Giganto's teeth by paleontologists shows that, just like other primates, the giant ape had four types of teeth: **incisors, canines, premolars,** and **molars.**

At the back of each side of the upper and lower jaws were three huge crushing molars. In front of the molars were three slightly smaller crushers, the premolars. The molars and premolars combined to form a powerful grinding machine able to pulverize the toughest bamboo shoots. In front of each premolar was a single canine tooth. Unlike the fearsome pointed canines found in gorillas, Giganto's canines were small and looked more like little premolars. Finally, in front of each canine was a pair of little peglike incisors. Giganto's canines and incisors combined to form an effective nipper, perfect for snipping off pieces of bamboo.

All in all, Giganto's teeth were just what the ape needed to live on a diet of bamboo and other tough grasses.

that Giganto, like the gorilla, must have a large sagittal crest on the top of its skull to serve as an anchor point for those huge jaw muscles.

Another interesting bit of information has come to light during the study of Giganto's teeth. All of the types of teeth in Giganto's mouth come in one of two sizes: either huge or extra huge. In gorillas and orangutans, adult males are much larger and stronger than adult females, and they have much larger teeth. This suggests that the larger Giganto teeth belonged to adult males, while the smaller teeth belonged to adult females. It also suggests that adult male Gigantos were a lot bigger and stronger than the females. (These differences between male and female Gigantos are examples of what scientists call **sexual dimorphism**. Dimorphism means "two forms.") Such a difference in body size usually means that the big males compete against each other over the smaller female mates. Can you imagine two 1,200-pound apes tussling to be king of the mountain? Professional wrestling would be nothing by comparison!

Because of its size and diet, scientists believe Giganto had a lot in common with other large plant-eaters such as elephants and rhinos. These animals eat lots of leafy plant material—such as grasses and tree leaves—and they eat them in large amounts. If this picture of Giganto is correct, then the giant ape was a bit of a slowpoke that spent most of its time lumbering around looking for food and stuffing itself with bamboo and fruit. It is quite a contrast to that speedy skunk ape from Florida.

Unfortunately, one important detail that cannot be determined from Giganto's jawbone and teeth is whether the giant ape walked on its hind legs, or whether it was a knuckle-walker like the gorilla. Even though Giganto most likely could have stood up and walked on two feet, at least for a short distance, many primate experts think it was a knuckle-walker. If Bigfoot were a modern version of Giganto, this would mean that Bigfoot is probably a knuckle-walker as well.

It should also be pointed out that the structure of Giganto's teeth suggest that its closest living relative is that other large Asian ape, the orangutan. But unlike the orangutan, which tops the scales at 200 pounds (90 kg), Giganto could not swing from trees. Weighing in at a half a ton, Giganto was much too heavy to swing on tree branches. On the rare occasions when orangutans venture to the ground, they knuckle-walk like gorillas and occasionally use their long arms like crutches, swinging their short-legged bodies along as they go. Orangutans are slow moving—by far the slowest of the apes. Unlike chimps and gorillas, which can run on all fours, orangutans don't run, probably because their legs are so much shorter than their arms. It's entirely possible that Giganto was every bit as slow as his little cousin.

A PUZZLE OR TWO

Assume for a moment that Bigfoot does indeed exist and that he is a descendant of Giganto. There are then a couple of puzzles to solve. First, Giganto lived in Asia, but Bigfoot lives in North America. So how did the giant ape get from there to here? Second, Giganto is now extinct, but Bigfoot is still around. Why did Bigfoot survive after Giganto disappeared?

As it turns out, neither of these puzzles is all that hard to solve.

Let's tackle the geography problem first: How could Giganto get from Asia to North America? During the Pleistocene Epoch, Earth's climate was colder than it is today. In fact, a major Ice Age occurred during this time in Earth's history. Water that evaporated from the ocean fell as snow on top of glaciers in the Northern Hemisphere, building up to the incredible depth of 1.2 miles (2 km). As the glaciers grew, the sea level dropped by as much as 330 feet (100 m). As a result, much land that had been drowned beneath the ocean waters ended up high and dry, well above sea level.

One area of land that became exposed by the lowered sea level was located between Alaska in North America and Siberia in northern Asia. It is now known as the Bering Land Bridge because it was located in the region of the Pacific Ocean known as the Bering Sea. The bridge was a corridor of dry land that allowed animals to gradually expand their range over the course of many generations and hundreds, if not thousands, of years, from one continent to the other.

The fossil record shows that plants grew on the land bridge, providing food for mammoths, bison, and other big, hairy herbivores as they made their way from Asia to North America. Since those animals made the trek, it is possible that big, hairy Giganto did, too. Once there, Giganto could then head east and south, on into Canada and the United States. There, it could start a new life with a new address and a new name: Sasquatch.

Now, the second puzzle: Why would Giganto become extinct in Asia, while Bigfoot survived in America? There are a number of possible explanations. First, there's the problem with bamboo, Giganto's main food. Bamboo occasionally dies off over large areas, leading to widespread starvation among animals that rely on it for food. In fact, many giant pandas, which depend on bamboo just as Giganto did, starved to death when massive amounts of bamboo forest died off in the 1970s. Pandas were Pleistocene neighbors of Giganto and undoubtedly competed with the giant ape for food, especially when bamboo was in short supply.

To top it all off, another primate, *Homo erectus* (an ancestor of our own species), used bamboo for food and to make tools. It may actually have hunted the big ape, too. Fossil evidence clearly shows that ancient members of our own species, *Homo sapiens*, killed and ate Giganto's little cousin, the orangutan. Therefore, it's conceivable that *H. erectus* killed and ate Giganto.

Scientists believe that Giganto became extinct in Asia because of a combination of these factors: an unreliable food source that sometimes died off, competition for that food from pandas and primitive people, and hunting pressure from humans. Perhaps, though, a few of the giant apes escaped across the Bering Land Bridge to North America, where they found new foods, didn't have competition from giant pandas (which stayed put in Asia), and learned to play a good game of hide-and-seek with human hunters, who also followed the Bering Land Bridge to America.

Of course, this scenario is based on pure guesswork. Following the end of the Pleistocene Ice Age, the glaciers melted and the sea levels rose once again, covering the Bering Land Bridge with water. Any Giganto fossils that may exist there are now out of reach, deep under the ocean. Scientists have found skeletal remains of ancient humans whose ancestors may have crossed the land bridge into northwestern North America, but no Giganto fossils have been found anywhere in the New World. Still, Giganto *could* have traveled from Asia to America during the Pleistocene Ice Age, and the ape *could* be the ancestor of Bigfoot—if, that is, Bigfoot really exists.

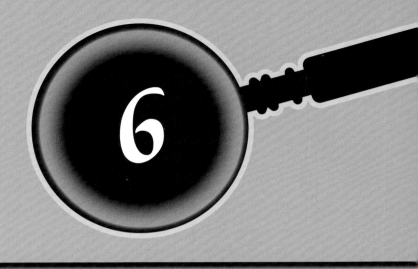

THE YETI AND THE YOWIE

tories of mysterious, hairy giants are not confined to the United States and Canada. In fact, all the continents—except uninhabited Antarctica—have their own versions of Bigfoot. Cultures from Africa, South America, Australia, Asia, and Europe (remember Grendel) are full of both modern eyewitness accounts and ancient folklore. These stories tell of huge humanlike apes or ape-like humans with extraordinary strength and special powers. They are creatures living on the edges of both the real landscape and the human imagination.

Of all the ape-men that appear to inhabit Earth, three stand out from all the rest. The first of them is Bigfoot. As will quickly become clear, the other two have a lot in common with their famous North American cousin. Many

Bigfoot researchers believe this is strong evidence that all three of these beasts exist. They feel that all the man-ape sightings that have been reported here and abroad cannot be explained as a worldwide case of mistaken identity. They are convinced that there must be some substance—in the form of a half-ton hulking beast—behind all those stories. With that in mind, let's take a look at Bigfoot's relatives, the Yeti and the Yowie.

THE YETI

In 1951, Eric Shipton, a member of a scientific expedition to the Himalaya Mountains, stumbled across a jaw-dropping discovery high up in the no-man's land of snow-covered mountain peaks in the world's tallest mountain chain. At 18,000 feet (5,500 m) up in the mountains, Shipton and his partner, Michael Ward, found a long trail of footprints plodding through deep snow at the edge of a glacier. The extraordinary part wasn't the mere presence of animal prints so high in the mountains. Bears, snow leopards, and other animals were already known to visit and leave tracks in such frigid, snowy places. What was so amazing about this particular set of tracks was the fact that they looked like nothing the two experienced outdoorsmen had ever seen before.

The trail was clearly made by a bipedal animal, because there were left and right footprints, one after the other. The big toe was long and thick, and it was **opposable**. Like a thumb on a hand, an opposable toe would allow the animal to grab objects with its foot the way a hand can. The remaining toes were much shorter, thinner, and clumped together, making the outline of the print look a bit like a big, fat mitten, 12.5 inches long and 7.5 inches wide (32 cm long and 19 cm wide). The prints had a definite primate look to them. In fact, they were similar to the smaller, skinnier foot of the sifaka lemur, a primate from Madagascar. (You might recognize a sifaka if you saw one: Zoboo, the lemur puppet on the popular TV show *Zoboomafoo*, is a sifaka.) Sifakas spend most of their time in trees, leaping and climbing from branch to branch; their opposable big toes help them clamber about. But they usually walk on two feet when on the ground. The mitten-style foot is suited to getting around both ways.

Shipton took photographs of one footprint that was in especially good condition. When those photos were published, the Yeti (dubbed "Abominable Snowman" by the tabloids) suddenly became something more than just a legend. Many people viewed that footprint as evidence that the Yeti was a real animal.

A number of Yeti-hunting expeditions were mounted as a result of Shipton's footprint photos, including one sponsored by World Book Encyclopedia. As is the case with Bigfoot, though, the Yeti always managed to stay one step ahead of its pursuers. Nevertheless, according to zoologist Edward Cronin, eyewitness descriptions provided by local people and Western explorers give a pretty clear and steady picture of what the creature looks like:

"Its body is stocky, apelike in shape, with a distinctly human quality to it, in contrast to that of a bear. It stands five and a half to six feet tall [1.7 to 1.8 m], and is covered with short, coarse hair, reddish brown to black in color, sometimes with white patches on the chest. The hair is longest on the shoulders. The face is hairless and rather flat. The jaw is robust, the teeth are quite large, though fangs are not present, and the mouth is wide. The head is conically shaped, and comes to a pointed crown. The arms are long, reaching almost to the knees. The shoulders are heavy and hunched. There is no tail."

Except for its size, the Yeti sounds a lot like Bigfoot. The fact that the Yeti is described as being smaller than Bigfoot

This picture was taken at 18,000 feet (5,500 m) in the mountains of Nepal. The explorers who discovered the footprints believe that they were left by the mysterious and elusive Yeti.

actually fits the fossil evidence. Think back to Giganto for a moment. The variety of Giganto that many cryptozoologists believe was Bigfoot's ancestor wasn't the only species of its kind. The suspected forefather of Bigfoot was *Gigantopithecus blacki* (abbreviated *G. blacki*), but there was another, smaller species of Giganto. The mandible and some teeth of this smaller species, *Gigantopithecus giganteus* (abbreviated *G. giganteus*), were found in northern India, near the Himalayas. It was bigger than a gorilla, but noticeably smaller than *G. blacki*.

If *G. giganteus* was an ancestor of the Yeti in the same way that *G. blacki* was an ancestor of Bigfoot, then the Yeti should be smaller than Bigfoot. That is exactly what appears to be the case. Also, the lack of fangs in *G. giganteus* is important. Unlike gorillas, whose canine teeth are long and fanglike, neither the Yeti nor Bigfoot reportedly has such long canines. This is in keeping with their supposed relationship to Giganto, cousin to the orangutan, which has short canines.

The Yeti appears to avoid contact with people, just like Bigfoot. Some people believe that this secretive creature lives in hidden river valley forests tucked away in the great mountains. If that's the case, why do people find Yeti footprints thousands of feet farther up the mountain slopes, marching along barren, snow-covered mountain glaciers? Edward Cronin stumbled across the answer to that question during his Himalayan expedition. At one point, Cronin and three colleagues decided to explore the high mountain slopes towering above the Himalayan valley forests. One night the group camped out in a small snow-covered field far up Mt. Kongma La. When they awoke the next morning, they discovered a set of tracks in the snow—tracks that weren't there the evening before. Looking at the footprints, it became clear that these prints looked a lot like the one in the Shipton photo.

The animal's tracks led right between the party's two tents. Following the trail, Cronin discovered that the Yeti had climbed up the north slope from one valley forest, crossed through the camp site (as if to check it out), and then gone down the south slope, heading toward another valley forest far below. The Yeti had simply taken a shortcut up and over a mountain ridge to get from one valley to the next—perhaps to look for a fresh supply of food—instead of taking a much longer route down and around the base of the mountain.

Unlike the case with Bigfoot, some Yeti seekers claim to have found actual Yeti spoor. Many monasteries in the Himalayas possess sacred Yeti scalps. At least, those are the claims of the monks who live there. One such scalp was borrowed for scientific analysis. The result? The source of the scalp could not be determined. The first study of the skin identified it as belonging to a serow, a goat native to the Himalayas. Further examination, however, revealed that remains of fleas and other insects found on the skin were not those normally found on serows. This is important, because individual species of those kinds of insects tend to only live on one particular species of animal. The fact that the insects found on the skin were not normally on serows suggests that the skin itself did not come from a serow. If not, then maybe it did come from the head of a Yeti. Unfortunately, since no one has ever captured a live Yeti, no one knows what kinds of insects it attracts. And so, the mystery of the Yeti continues. . . .

THE YOWIE

On to Australia, the land of the Yowie. Descriptions of the Yowie are remarkably similar to those of Bigfoot and the Yeti. Compare the following general description of Yowies given by Australian cryptozoologists Tony Healy and Paul Cropper with what we know about the Yeti and Bigfoot:

Some monasteries in the Himalayas have what monks claim to be scalps of the Yeti. They may be the skin of the serow, a type of goat. In this photo, a monk displays one of the alleged Yeti scalps.

"Yowies resemble huge apelike men or manlike apes. They are frequently likened to long-legged gorillas. A full-grown adult is seven and a half to eight feet tall [2.3 to 2.4 m] and very heavily built; covered from head to foot in dark hair; its dome-shaped head may seem small in comparison to its very wide, but rounded, shoulders; skin is brown to black; eyes large and deep-set; ears small, set close to side of head; nose flat; mouth wide, lips thin; teeth large and fearsome; upper canines sometimes protrude over the lower lip; neck extremely short and thick; arms very long and muscular; hands roughly humanlike with very strong nails or claws; legs as long, proportionately, as those of a human."

All three of these creatures look like huge, dark-haired, no-necked, dome-headed, long-armed, flat-nosed ape-men (although the Yeti appears smaller than the other two). Like its North American cousin, the Yowie sometimes stinks horribly. Rotten garbage and vomit are among the most common descriptions, along with colorful references to such smelly stuff as burning mattresses, dirty hen houses, and bat caves.

Most Yowie sightings have occurred along the Great Dividing Range, a rugged mountain range that runs parallel to most of the east coast of Australia, roughly 50 to 100 miles (80 to 160 km) inland from the Pacific Ocean. The mountains in this Yowie stronghold are very rocky and steep-sloped and are covered with dense forests and bushy scrub. Few people venture into them. But because many towns and cities (including Sydney, Australia's largest city, with more than 4 million people) are located along the nearby coast, Yowie sightings are common in that part of the country.

Many Yowie sightings take place in backyards and along roadways, not in the wilderness. In fact, Yowies seem to be downright inquisitive, peeking in windows and spying on people working or playing outdoors. Many people walking, running, or horseback riding along the road have glimpsed Yowies running right along with them in the nearby woods, giving themselves away with the crackling sound of their footsteps on the forest floor.

Like their Bigfoot cousin, Yowies are often noisy, making sounds ranging from huffs and roars to snarls and screams. Also like Bigfoot, Yowies seem to have glow-in-the-dark eyes, usually red but sometimes yellow. Plus, as is the case with both Bigfoot and the Yeti, hardly anyone ever comes across Yowie droppings. This is kind of odd, considering how big these animals are and how much food they must eat.

One man has been lucky enough (or perhaps *un*lucky, considering the smell) to come across what might be an actual Yowie dropping. It was a fresh deposit, and according to Healy and Cropper, "the massive object was still hot and steaming" when the man found it. It was unbelievably stinky, and it was huge: 18 inches long (46 cm) and about 2.5 inches (6 cm) in diameter. It had lots of plant and insect remains in it (especially beetles and grubs), but no hair or bones. The presence of insect remains in the dropping is significant, because Yowies reportedly use their fangs to pry off chunks of tree bark to get at tasty beetle grubs hiding inside.

Perhaps the most unusual aspect of Yowie biology is the animal's feet. Foot and footprint descriptions supplied by Yowie witnesses are even more varied than those of Bigfoot. These descriptions include everything from pretty normal, five-toed feet to three-toed versions with long claws, to webbed monstrosities resembling starfish, to others that have the toes actually pointing backward instead of forward. Some of these sightings are obviously the product of overactive imaginations, but others are quite similar to some Bigfoot prints, which suggests that these two creatures might be the same type of animal.

LET'S GET TECHNICAL: THE HOBBITS OF FLORES

*A*ccording to modern residents of the island of Flores, a population of little furry people lived on their island as recently as 300 years ago. If that's true, it's possible that some of these little hairy humans colonized Australia during the Pleistocene Ice Age. At that time, the lowered sea levels exposed several low-lying islands across which the tiny primate could have "hop-scotched." It may have used rafts of floating vegetation flushed out to sea during floods or tsunamis, for example. In this way, it could have traveled from Flores to Australia, where it became known as the Junjudee. The Yowie, possibly a descendant of *Gigantopithecus*, may have likewise jumped from Asia to Australia during the Ice Age.

At first, there was some argument among anthropologists as to whether the remains of these "hobbits" (as the Western world has nicknamed little *Homo floresiensis*) actually represent a new species. Some anthropologists argued that these specimens were from a pygmylike tribe of *Homo sapiens*, or were perhaps people afflicted with a condition known as microcephaly, characterized by an abnormally small head. As additional fossil remains have surfaced, however, the status of *Homo floresiensis* as a distinct species is now more certain.

Any discussion of the Yowie wouldn't be complete without mentioning Australia's other ape-man. That's right: Australia has the distinction of having *two* hairy ape-men. But this second creature is just a little guy, barely 3 feet tall (1 m). Called the Junjudee by aborigines (Native Australians), this cryptid is especially interesting because a few fossils of a tiny species of human, *Homo floresiensis*, were recently found on the island of Flores, located just over 400 miles (640 km) north of Australia.

A *Homo floresiensis* skull (*left*) is shown next to a human skull. The *Homo floresienses* skull is believed to be 18,000 years old.

Some Yowie experts speculate that Junjudees may be descendants of these little people. Unfortunately, despite their small size, they have managed to avoid direct contact with their larger human cousins, just as the Yowie has.

FINAL REPORT ON BIGFOOT

*I*t's time to wrap up the investigation here. All the data have been collected and analyzed, and a brief summary of the findings is now in order.

The stories of Ape Canyon, Bluff Creek, and the Albert Ostman kidnapping are of limited use in this investigation. No solid evidence backs up any of these stories. In particular, Ray Wallace's reputation as a jokester weakens all the evidence collected at the road construction site at Bluff Creek. That includes Jerry Crew's impressive plaster footprint cast. The odd details of Ostman's story of his adventure cast a big cloud of doubt over his tale, too. All three of these tales make for entertaining reading, but that's as far as they go. None of them is of much value to serious Bigfoot researchers on the trail of Sasquatch.

The William Roe story is also not very useful as a source of Bigfoot information, because, once again, there's no solid evidence to verify that Roe's Bigfoot encounter actually happened. Roe's story does have some value, though. The similarity between parts of his tale and the sequence of events in Roger Patterson's Bigfoot film suggests that Roe's story may have served as the script for Patterson's little movie.

With the Roger Patterson film, just what can cryptozoologists conclude about the rodeo rider's brief claim to fame? Is Patty real? Or is she Bob Heironimus in an ape costume? Cryptozoologists don't know. The movie is too blurry to tell one way or the other, and with no costume in hand, even the most hard-nosed skeptic can't prove beyond all doubt that the movie is a hoax. Final judgment for Case #1: inconclusive.

What about the other cases in *CSI: Bigfoot*? Case #2, the Minnesota Iceman, can be laid to rest with one word: fake. The Iceman was a clever hoax played by a master of deception, and Frank Hansen should receive recognition for that. But the Iceman's value to Bigfoot researchers is absolutely nothing. Final judgment for Case #2: hoax.

Case #3, Cripple Foot, is an interesting one. It started out looking like a real case of a close encounter with Bigfoot. Anthropologists Grover Krantz and John Napier were both taken in by it, assuming no hoaxer could possibly know enough about feet to fake a correct Bigfoot clubfoot. But a hoaxer doesn't need detailed knowledge of clubfoot anatomy to make a fake clubfoot. All that's needed is a photograph of one. Furthermore, the involvement of Ivan Marx, who was shown by Peter Byrne to be a Bigfoot hoaxer, leads to one clear final judgment: hoax.

Finally, we come to the mud puddle at Skookum Meadows, Case #4. All the evidence points to the Skookum body print being made by an elk. Yet BFRO investigators continue to believe that a big, hairy primate made the print.

A 15-inch footprint was discovered in the foothills of the Blue Mountains of southeastern Washington in 1996 by Paul Freeman, and photographed by Jeff Meldrum.

Wishful thinking influenced the judgment of Ivan Sanderson and Bernard Heuvelmans when they examined the Iceman, and that may be the case here, too. The Skookum investigators could be letting their eagerness to find Bigfoot influence their interpretation of the evidence. Final judgment for Case #4: mistaken identity. An elk, not Bigfoot, made the body print.

This investigation has uncovered major problems with the evidence behind each of the Bigfoot believers' strongest cases. Has it proved that Bigfoot doesn't exist? No. It has simply shown, by separating fact from fiction, and reality from wishful thinking, that no one has proved that Bigfoot *does* exist. But who knows what the future will bring? There's always a chance, however small, that someone will obtain that proof tomorrow . . . or next week . . . or next year.

If these animals do exist, perhaps it has been difficult to find them because there are so very few of them. Those in existence may be part of small populations scrambling to stay alive by avoiding contact with anything that might pose a threat to their survival. Humans—those beings running noisy construction sites, cutting down trees, and exploding dynamite— would definitely be seen as a threat by an animal with any sort of intelligence.

Still, admitting the possibility that Bigfoot exists is one thing, while proving that Bigfoot exists is a whole different ballgame. Proof requires evidence that no one can disprove. That's the kind of evidence we looked for in all of these cases. Unfortunately, the search came up short. The solid evidence wasn't there. The burden of proof rests on the shoulders of the Bigfoot believers. Obviously, their work is not done.

TWO POINTS TO PONDER

Before closing the book on Bigfoot, here are a couple of points to ponder: First of all, think back to those old Native American totem poles from the Pacific Northwest. Clearly, an apelike creature played a part in the culture of these Americans. But does that mean such a creature actually lived in the nearby mountain forests? Not necessarily. What if these people's ancestors brought *Gigantopithecus* along with them as they crossed the Bering Land Bridge from Asia to North America—not the actual animal, but the *memory* of the animal from the distant past? It could be a bit of folklore passed down through the generations, extending all the way back to the time when the human ancestor *Homo erectus* lived alongside the giant ape in the bamboo forests of Asia. It's a fascinating idea, because it suggests that two species, separated by 200,000 years and thousands of miles, share a common bond through their culture. If Seeahtlks and Dzonoqua represent ancient folklore creatures rather than real animals, then that would certainly explain why no one has been able to prove that the hairy beast actually exists.

Finally, on a much lighter note, consider bogus Bigfoot feet one last time. Among Ray Wallace's collection of Bigfoot paraphernalia were fake feet that had a curious indentation along the edge of the ball of the foot, forming a so-called double-ball. The double-ball footprint is unique to Bigfoot and has become somewhat of a Bigfoot trademark, even though many alleged Bigfoot prints lack this feature. Knowing what a jokester Wallace was, it's tempting to believe that he used the double-ball as a sort of secret signature. And an appropriate one it would have been: The outline of the double ball from a fake left footprint looks suspiciously like a capital *B*. *B* as in *Bigfoot*. What do you think?

GLOSSARY

Abominable   Causing a feeling of disgust or hatred

Achilles tendon   A thick, tough band that runs up the back of the foot and ankle and attaches the muscles of the foot and leg to the bones there

Anatomy   The study of the structure of organisms

Artifact: Something produced by human work (for example, pottery or arrowheads). It can also be an artificially or unintentionally produced change in appearance (for example, desiccation ridges produced in footprint casts).

Authentic   Real or genuine

Bioluminescence   The act of giving off light from the body by living things

Bipedal   Walking on two feet. Humans and apes are bipedal.

Canine   The tooth located just behind the incisors at the front of the jaw

Cast   An object shaped in a mold. A footprint cast is made by pouring liquid plaster into the footprint, and then removing the plaster in one piece after it has hardened.

Cryptid   An unknown animal that some people believe exists, even though there is not enough evidence to prove its existence

Cryptozoology   The study of unknown animals

Dermatoglyph   The complicated pattern of tiny ridges and valleys found on the palms, fingers, feet, and toes of primates. Those on fingers are commonly known as fingerprints.

Femur   The upper leg bone

Folklore   Beliefs and stories shared by a group of people

Forensics   The use of science and technology to investigate and establish facts in a court of law

Genus   A group of closely related species

Herbivore   A plant-eating animal

Humerus   The upper arm bone

Incisor   One of the small teeth located at the very front of the jaw. There are two incisors on each side of each jaw.

Molar   The large crushing tooth at the back of the jaw. There are three molars on each side of both jaws.

Mold   A hollow shape in which something is formed to make a cast

Nocturnal   Active during the night. Owls and bats are examples of nocturnal animals.

Opposable   Able to be used opposite something else, in order to grab an object. A hand's opposable thumb allows it to grab objects between the thumb and fingers.

Paleontologist   A scientist who studies fossils

Pace   How fast a person or animal walks or moves

Photophore   An organ or structure that contains light-producing bacteria

Phytolith   A particle of the mineral silica contained in the cells of many plants. Phytoliths make plant leaves tough to eat.

Pleistocene Epoch   The period in Earth's history extending from 1.8 million years ago to 11,000 years ago

Premolar   The small crushing teeth located between the molars and canine tooth. There are three premolars on each side of both jaws.

Primate   The group of mammals that includes monkeys, apes, lemurs, lorises, and their relatives. Humans are primates.

Quadrupedal   Walking on four feet. Dogs and cats are examples of quadrupeds.

Radius   The short, thick bone of the forearm

Sagittal crest   A vertical ridge of bone that extends down the middle of the top of a gorilla's skull. The crest serves as an attachment site for the large muscles of the jaw.

Sexual dimorphism   The condition in which males and females of an animal species have different characteristics, such as adult body size, presence or absence of antlers, etc.

Skeptic   A person who uses science and reason, rather than wishful thinking or gut feelings, to draw a conclusion.

Species   A single type of animal or plant, such as the orang-utan. Closely related species are grouped together into a genus.

Specimen   An example of a plant, animal, or mineral

Spoor   The track or trail of a wild animal

Tibia   The thick lower leg bone, also called the shinbone

Walking cycle   A series of two complete steps: a left footstep followed by right footstep

Zoologist   A scientist who studies animals

BIBLIOGRAPHY

Arsuaga, Juan Luis and I. Martínez. *The Chosen Species: The Long March of Human Evolution*. Malden, Mass.: Blackwell Publishing, 1998.

Baird, Don. "Bigfoot: Fabricating Sasquatch Footprint." Bigfoot-encounters.com. Available online. URL: http://www.bigfootencounters.com/biology/baird.htm. Accessed April 27, 2008.

Byrne, Peter. *The Search for Bigfoot: Monster, Myth or Man?* Washington, D.C.: Acropolis Books Ltd., 1975.

Ciochon, Russell L. "The Ape that Was." Ebscohost.com. Available online. URL: http://web.ebscohost.com/ehost/detail?vid=3&hid=105&sid=ad744c34-1fad-41cc-99950b5a4ea4dd06%40sessionmgr109. Accessed May 25, 2008.

Ciochon, Russell, J. Olsen, and J. James. *Other Origins: The Search for the Giant Ape in Human Prehistory*. New York: Bantam Books, 1990.

"Clubfoot." *Encyclopedia of Children's Health: Infancy Through Adolescence*. Available online. URL: www.healthofchildren.com/C/Clubfoot.html. Accessed April 27, 2008.

Coleman, Loren. *Bigfoot: The True Story of Apes in America*. New York: Paraview Pocket Books, 2003.

Coleman, Loren. *M. K. Davis: Bigfoot Has Ponytail*. Cryptomundo.com. Available online. URL: http://www.cryptomundo.com/cryptozoo-news/bf-ponytail/. Accessed June 25, 2008.

Cronin, Edward W., Jr. *The Arun: A Natural History of the World's Deepest Valley*. Boston: Houghton Mifflin Company, 1979.

Cronin, Edward W., Jr. "The Yeti." *Atlantic Monthly* 236, no. 5 (1975): 45–47.

Crowley, Matt. "Dermal Ridges and Casting Artifacts." Orgoneresearch.com. Available online. URL: http://www.orgoneresearch.com/dermalridges.htm. Accessed April 27, 2008.

Daegling, David J. *Bigfoot Exposed: An Anthropologist Examines America's Enduring Legend.* Walnut Creek, Calif.: Altamira Press, 2004.

Dennett, Michael R. "Experiments Cast Doubt on Bigfoot 'Evidence.'" Skeptical Briefs. Available online. URL: http://www.csicop.org/sb/2006-09/bigfoot.html. Accessed April 27, 2008.

Duck Soup. VHS. Universal City, Calif.: MCA Home Video, 1995.

Dunbar, Robin and L. Barrett. *Cousins: Our Primate Relatives.* London: BBC Worldwide Ltd., 2000.

Futuyma, Douglas J. *Evolution.* Sunderland, Mass.: Sinauer Associates, 2005.

Green, John. *Sasquatch: The Apes Among Us.* Seattle, Wa.: Hancock House Publishers, 1978.

Healy, Tony and P. Cropper. *The Yowie: In Search of Australia's Bigfoot.* San Antonio, Tex.: Anomalist Books, 2006.

Kehoe, Alice Beck. *Controversies in Archaeology.* Walnut Creek, Calif.: Left Coast Press, 2008.

Long, Greg. *The Making of Bigfoot.* Amherst, N.Y.: Prometheus Books, 2004.

Loxton, Daniel. "Bigfoot Part One: Dawn of Sasquatch." *Skeptic* 11, no. 2 (2004): 97–105.

Loxton, Daniel. "Bigfoot Part Two: The Case for the Sasquatch." *Skeptic* 11, no. 3 (2005): 96–105.

Meldrum, Jeff. *Sasquatch: Legend Meets Science.* New York: Tom Doherty Associates, 2006.

Muir, John Kenneth. *Horror Films of the 1970s.* Jefferson, N.C.: McFarland and Company, 2002.

Napier, John. *Bigfoot: The Yeti and Sasquatch in Myth and Reality.* London: Jonathan Cope, 1972.

Pyle, Robert Michael. *Where Bigfoot Walks: Crossing the Dark Divide.* Boston: Houghton Mifflin Company, 1995.

Radford, Benjamin. "Bigfoot at 50: Evaluating a Half-Century of Bigfoot Evidence." *Skeptical Inquirer* 26, no. 2 (2002): 29–34.

Radford, Benjamin. "The Nonsense and Non-science of Sasquatch." *Skeptical Inquirer* 31 no. 3 (2007): 58–59.

Reynolds, Vernon. *The Apes: The Gorilla, Chimpanzee, Orangutan, and Gibbon—Their History and Their World*. New York: E.P. Dutton & Co, 1967.

Sasquatch: Legend Meets Science. DVD. Coon Rapids, Minn.: Whitewolf Entertainment, Inc., 2002.

Sever, Megan. "More 'Hobbits' in Indonesia." *Geotimes* 50, no. 12 (2005): 37.

"Zoboomafoo." Wikipedia. Available online. URL: http://en.wikipedia.org/wiki/Zoboomafoo. Accessed April 27, 2008.

FURTHER RESOURCES

Bigfoot and Other Monsters. VHS. New York: A&E Television Networks, 2001.

Coleman, Loren and Patrick Huyghe. *The Field Guide to Bigfoot, Yeti, and Other Mystery Primates Worldwide*. New York: Avon Books, 1999.

Innes, Brian. *Giant Humanlike Beasts*. Austin, Tex.: Raintree Steck-Vaughn Publishers, 1999.

Krantz, Grover. *Bigfoot/Sasquatch Evidence*. Surrey, B.C.: Hancock House, 1999.

Sanderson, Ivan T. *Abominable Snowmen: Legend Come to Life*. Kempton, Ill.: Adventures Unlimited Press, 2006.

WEB SITES

Australian Yowie Research
http://www.yowiehunters.com/index.php?option=com_frontpage&Itemid=1
The official Web site of the Australian Yowie Research organization. Contains many eyewitness accounts of Yowie sightings.

Bigfoot: Fact or Fancy?
http://home.clara.net/rfthomas/classics/bluffc.html
This Bigfoot Web site contains detailed accounts of the most famous Bigfoot stories, along with a listing of Bigfoot sightings in the United States.

Bigfoot Field Researchers Organization
http://www.bfro.net
This is the official Web site of the Bigfoot Field Researchers Organization, a group of cryptozoologists that gather information about Bigfoot.

Cryptozoology.com
http://www.cryptozoology.com/cryptids/sasquatch.php
This cryptozoology Web site gives detailed descriptions of many cryptids, including Bigfoot.

Sasquatch Information Society
http://www.bigfootinfo.org
The site contains a database of Bigfoot and Yeti sightings, as well as a collection of recent Bigfoot news articles.

Yeti: Abominable Snowman of the Himalayas
http://unmuseum.mus.pa.us/yeti.htm
This is the Yeti Web page in Unmuseum.org, an online museum about cryptids, UFOs, and other unexplained phenomena.

PICTURE CREDITS

INDEX

ABOUT THE AUTHOR

RICK EMMER is a substitute science and math teacher for the Avon Lake City School District in northeast Ohio. He was previously an aquarist at the Cleveland Aquarium and a zookeeper at the Cleveland Metroparks Zoo. Emmer has a bachelor's degree in biology from Mount Union College and a master's degree in biology from John Carroll University. He was a member of the International Society of Cryptozoology for several years. Emmer lives with his family in Bay Village, Ohio, smack dab in the middle of Cryptid Country, with the lair of the Lake Erie Monster to the north and the hideout of the Grassman, Ohio's Bigfoot, to the south.